CUSHIONS AND COVERS

CUSHIONS AND COVERS

SUE LOCKE

WARD LOCK

ACKNOWLEDGEMENTS

The publishers would like to thank the following for allowing photographs to be reproduced in this book: All paints by Dulux, page 74; Elizabeth Whiting & Associates, pages 15, 27, 34, 38, 42 and 66; Michael Boys Syndication, pages 43, 50, 55 and 63; Hand-painted units by Smallbone Kitchens/Tiled splashback by Paris Ceramics, page 22.

First published in Great Britain in 1989
by Ward Lock, Villiers House, 41/47 Strand, London WC2N 5JE

First paperback edition 1990.

A Cassell imprint.

Text filmset in Bauer Bodoni
by Facet Film Composing Ltd, Leigh-on-Sea, Essex

Printed and bound in Spain by Graficas Reunidas

British Library Cataloguing in Publication Data
Locke, Sue
    Cushions and covers.
    1. Soft furnishings. Making — Manuals
    1. Title
    646.2′1

ISBN 0–7063–6911–4

CONTENTS

These eye-catching bolster cushions, which have been made to look like crackers, contrast with the plain bed cover

PART I

1 THE PERSONAL TOUCH

The most important aspect of furnishing a home is that you should feel entirely comfortable with the end result. Magazines and books may inspire you to re-think your ideas but however you choose to furnish a room it should reflect your personality.

Although cushions and covers are considered to be the finishing touches to a room, they can become the focal point and their importance should not be overlooked. A plain sofa can be transformed by the addition of several brightly-coloured cushions. A rather worn suite can be brought right up to date with a loose cover in a stunning modern print.

Today, when so much of our furniture is mass produced, you can run the risk of living in a home that is identical to those of your friends and neighbours. Sewing your own cushions and covers can give your home that personal touch which makes all the difference.

CREATING THE RIGHT EFFECT

One of the first decisions to be made about furnishing a room is knowing the type of image you want to create. You might like to keep in mind the period of your house and whether you want to furnish it accordingly. A stone cottage is the perfect setting for floral prints in pretty colours; a modern flat, with its stark interior, would be complemented by simple modern furniture using strong geometric shapes and contrasting colours, such as black and white. Alternatively, you may opt for the challenge of creating a rustic country look in a modern flat or use simple stark furniture in your cottage. It is important to make a decision about the type of image you want and then to follow it through in all your rooms so that the decor blends together.

Having decided on the look you want to create you need to study the furniture you intend to cover. Does it have a stark severe line, or is the shape very round? Do you want to emphasize or disguise the shape? A simple stripe or bold geometric pattern will accentuate and complement the lines of a modern chair, and an intricate floral print can exaggerate the comfort of an over-stuffed sofa.

Another point worth considering is whether you need to use your furnishings to create an illusion. This is particularly relevant if you have a room that is especially low or narrow — striped fabrics can most effectively create an illusion of extra height or width.

COLOUR

Selecting fabrics can be very challenging. With such a wealth of colours, prints and textures to choose from it is quite easy for a state of panic to set in and then you can end up buying a 'total-look', from a shop which has co-ordinated wallpaper, with fabrics, paints, borders, china and every conceivable accessory. But shopping this way really takes the fun and excitement out of decorating a room. As a result you may well tire of the whole effect rather quickly.

The first major decision about colour is knowing the colour theme you intend to work with. It is very tempting to play safe and simply work with soft pastel shades, thus creating a rather dull and insipid setting. However, if your property is not over large you may consider having a basic colour used to a greater or lesser extent in every room. This creates an integrated colour scheme and a feeling of harmony and continuity. Remember that doors are often left open when one room is connected to another, so it is important to consider the colour schemes of neighbouring rooms in relation to the one you are currently furnishing. It is helpful to collect a scrap-book of design ideas and colour themes that you particularly like, storing them for future reference if need be. The main priority is to develop a very broad approach to colour and not be limited by those you feel safe with.

The colour wheel
Knowing which colours complement each other can be discovered by referring to the colour wheel (fig. 1). Essentially there are three basic colours, red, yellow and blue, from which all other colours come. Mixing these primary colours together creates secondary colours, e.g. blue and red making violet. Complementary colours are achieved by matching the secondary colour with the primary colour that has not been used to make it, so that violet would be complementary with yellow. Complementary colours provide the greatest degree of contrast. The remaining colours in the wheel are made up of equal

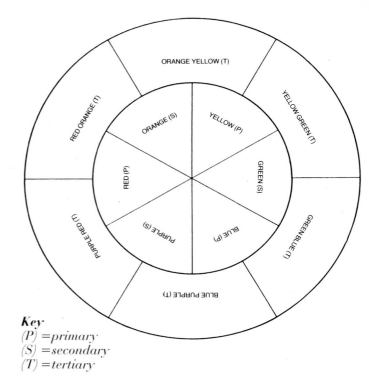

Key
(P) =primary
(S) =secondary
(T) =tertiary

1 *The colour wheel. When a primary and secondary colour are mixed a tertiary colour is produced*

parts of a primary colour and its closest secondary. Neighbouring colours such as violet and pink can be used for a more subtle effect. You might like to paint in the colours on a colour wheel, cut them into sections and, by laying them on top of each other, see how they react with one another. The more you experiment with colours the more knowledge you will gain, and this in turn creates confidence.

Neutral colours are black and white in the most extreme form, but can also include off-white, most of the browns, from beige to dark brown plus camel, also shades of grey, ranging from light silver through to charcoal.

Creating a mood

By working with certain colours you can create a definite mood in a room. In order to create a very cool atmosphere you can use shades of blue plus colours such as off-white, cream, sand, grey and light brown. To create a warm, welcoming room you need to think in terms of colours with yellow or gold properties, or a profusion of rich reds and deep blues. In creating a room with strong colour contrasts you can make a very lively and exciting atmosphere, choosing opposites such as red and green, blue and yellow or black and orange. You may like to take the effect of contrasting things a step further by placing the round curvy lines of flowers, either dried or fresh, alongside a geometrically shaped vase or light fitting. If a contrasting colour scheme is too bold for you, you may prefer to achieve a more integrated look by working with shapes and designs that can be blended together and colour combinations that are gentle and more subtle. Creating a quieter atmosphere may seem simple but success is judged by being able to combine various subtle prints together, without the finished room looking insipid and boring.

Having decided the colours you intend to use for your flooring, walls and ceiling try to keep a small colour swatch of each handy. Keep the swatches with you whenever you are shopping, so that if something catches your eye you can tell immediately whether it will add or detract from your chosen colour theme.

Try to avoid making the mistake of buying something simply because it looks good in someone else's home, or because it has been reduced in price. Bringing a book of swatches home is the most satisfactory way of selecting fabric, so that you are able to judge how the cloth looks away from the shop environment.

Light

By working with swatches of fabric at home you can judge how the cloth reacts to the light in the room you are furnishing. You may have a room with high ceilings that create a feeling of spaciousness and plenty of daylight. Alternatively, you may be limited to a dark narrow room. Colourwise, dark colours tend to make a room appear smaller while light ones create an illusion of extra space. A room that offers plenty of daylight has few drawbacks and you have the opportunity to combine a large number of different prints together. With a small room you need to decide whether you think it would be better to introduce lots of light bright prints to make it appear larger or whether by using rich warm colours you could create a very cosy setting.

Printed or plain?

The size of a room determines the quantity of printed or plain fabrics that you can use. In a small room too many prints can look very muddled, whereas just two or three set against a plain background will look stunning. With large rooms avoid using too many plain colours or the end result will be uninteresting and monotonous.

It is possible to assemble a variety of prints together in close proximity, provided they have at least one colour common to all of them. This might be a soft romantic floral design in different patterns but linked by the colour pink, blue or green. Alternatively, you might like to work with solid,

This delightful chair has a deep frill gathered onto the welt, contrasting white piping and white ribbon ties to secure the cover

bright, primary colours where perhaps a rich red or gold is incorporated on each of the prints you have chosen. If you are planning to bring a group of prints together, always work with swatches first, not by memory, so that you can be sure that all the prints will blend together.

A more harmonious effect is achieved by keeping patterns and furniture in scale with the size of the room. If you want to draw attention to a particular item of furniture, such as a favourite chair or sofa, you might consider using a dominant colour so that your eye is immediately drawn to that particular area of the room. Equally if you want to disguise another area avoid using a busy bright pattern. Choose instead a colour theme that will blend with your surrounding walls and carpet.

2 FABRICS & FILLINGS

FABRIC

Before selecting fabric consider the function of the room you are furnishing. In the kitchen, for example, use an easy-care fabric that can be thrown into a washing machine if food or drinks get spilt on it. You will need to bear this in mind, too, when choosing cushions and covers for dining areas. Washable fabrics are also more suitable for children's rooms where sticky hands are liable to wander over furnishings. If you have a young family and/or pets it is worth considering using *only* washable fabrics, so that you can feel more relaxed when youngsters or animals invade a newly-furnished room.

The swing ticket on the end of a roll of fabric will describe its particular properties. By studying it, you will discover the width of the fabric, washing or cleaning instructions and the fibre content. If you are unable to find a ticket or require more information, ask to speak to the department manager. It is never worth simply guessing whether a fabric is washable or not. A cloth that has been designed to be dry-cleaned only can be ruined by washing and many hours of careful work will be wasted.

Another point worth considering is whether plain light-coloured fabrics are advisable if you have an active family. Soft, subtle shades might look very attractive but a busy print or darker shade will disguise marks and stains more easily. Consider also just how much wear-and-tear your cushions or covers are likely to receive. Floor cushions and loose covers will require heavy-duty fabrics, whereas cushions and throwover covers, used for purely decorative purposes, can be made from delicate cloths such as satin or lace.

For a professional finish you will need to match patterns on a printed fabric which has a large motif, especially for loose covers and you will need to buy more material if you are using a cloth with a large pattern repeat rather than one which is plain or has an overall pattern.

It is not just colour and patterns that make fabric interesting — the texture of cloth is just as important. Consider whether you want to sit on something smooth and silky or would you prefer a natural, warmer-looking cloth which is perhaps rougher. For added interest it can be fun combining fabrics with different textures. Note that shiny fabrics tend to reflect light whereas rough coarse ones will absorb it affecting your overall scheme.

Your choice of texture might also be determined by other features in your room. Study the room and decide whether you want to echo or contrast with existing surfaces such as a rough brick fireplace, a shaggy rug or a glossy ceiling.

By studying fabrics with different textures you can begin to see how the fabric is constructed. A piece of cloth is made up of two types of thread, the warp and the weft. The warp is the stronger one. The weft runs from selvedge to selvedge (the selvedge is the finished edge of the cloth) and the weft thread is woven in and out of the warp thread. Warp threads are designed to take the strain on a piece of material.

Generally speaking, dress fabrics are not suitable for home furnishings. Firstly, they can be impractical as they are often only 90 cm (36 in) wide as opposed to furnishing fabrics at between 140/150 cm (56/60 in) wide. Secondly, they can be considerably more expensive. Cushions and covers designed for plenty of hard wear should be made from furnishing fabrics, but dress fabrics can be used for decorative items such as a bedroom throwover cover or cushions.

When shopping for fabric always buy the best quality you can afford and avoid being side-tracked by fancy names or designs.

Natural or man-made?

Natural fabrics are those made solely from natural fibres from animal or vegetable sources, whereas man-made ones are natural fibres that have been chemically treated (synthetic fibres are ones made entirely from chemicals). Both types of fabric have their advantages. Natural fabrics tend to respond well when cleaned but are more likely to shrink and crease. Man-made fabrics attract dirt more easily but they are unlikely to shrink and less likely to crease. The main groups of man-made fibres are acetate, acrylics, nylons and polyesters. The main groups of natural fibres are cotton, linen, wool and silk.

NATURAL FABRICS

Cotton

Cotton fabrics are very popular for home furnishing and have a traditional following. They are also extremely tough and can withstand plenty of rough treatment. However, cotton does have a tendency to shrink, so wash the fabric before you cut it. Also, if time is at a premium, cotton does require careful ironing. The following are the most popular cotton-based fabrics.

Brocade is a rich heavy-looking cloth that has a pattern woven into it. Cotton brocade is often woven with other yarns to give a silky pattern on a dullish background.

Bedford cord is often simply referred to as corduroy. This cloth is identified by the surface rib effect that can vary in width.

Calico is an inexpensive cloth that can be dyed or printed. It is used mainly for inner covers for cushions.

Chintz is a very popular choice for home furnishings. It has a glazed finish and is available in a printed or plain cloth.

Cretonne is a firmly-woven fabric not unlike chintz but without the glazed finish. The fabric is often reversible.

Damask is similar in weight to brocade. It usually features a matt pattern on a satin weave background.

Gingham is an inexpensive cloth, ideal for beginners. It can be cut on the cross for an effective finish. It is a very lightweight cloth only suitable for cushions or a bedroom throwover.

Lace is a delicate cloth where a pattern is applied to a mesh background, suitable only for decorative purposes.

Madras is a woven design fabric, often in a check or stripe, usually dyed in a variety of bright colours.

Sateen is a strong shiny fabric with a matt surface on the reverse side. It can be used for cushion inner covers and linings.

Ticking is a very strong fabric closely woven in twill, herringbone or satin weaves. It can often be found woven into stripes with coloured yarn. It is suitable for cushion inner covers provided the main fabric is not too sheer.

Velvet and velveteen are rich, soft-to-the-touch cloths that are ideal for formal chairs and sofas.

Linen

Linen, like cotton, is also a popular choice for loose covers. Although it can be expensive it is extremely hard-wearing. (Chintz, damask and brocade can be bought with a linen base.)

Wool

Woollen fabrics create a feeling of warmth, but wool fibres are not strong enough for most home-furnishing projects. However, light woollen cloths, frayed at the edges, may make attractive throwover covers for a sofa or chair. To make it more durable, wool is sometimes mixed with other fibres. Plush, a velour woollen fabric with a heavy pile is sometimes used in soft furnishings.

Silk

Silk-based fabrics have an air of luxury about them. Although silk is strong it is also very expensive so it is often mixed with other fibres.

Brocade can be bought as a silk-based fabric, often to be found with a silver or gold thread woven into it.

Crepe de Chine is a very soft silky fabric and can be used for a bedroom throwover cover or decorative cushions.

Taffeta and moiré are firmer types of silk fabric. Moiré can be identified by a ripple effect that seems to run across the surface of the cloth. Both are suitable for throwover covers or cushions.

Velvet can also be purchased with a silk base but it is expensive.

MAN-MADE FABRICS

Acetate is constructed by treating cotton linters. Like so many man-made fibres it is easy to care for and will not shrink. It can often be found in imitation silks such as brocades and moirés. Acetate is often combined with silk and cotton.

Acrylic is a bulky fabric with a soft quality. It has a resemblance to wool, and it is warm, strong and crease resistant. It is often mixed with other fabrics, such as wool or cotton.

Nylon is a by-product of coal. It is a strong but lightweight cloth, easy to use and hard to crease. Nylon can be drip-dried and requires little ironing. It is often mixed with other fibres and can be used for synthetic lace, net or satin — all are suitable for cushion covers or throwovers.

Polyester is a hard-wearing fabric often combined with other natural fabrics such as wool, silk, cotton or linen. It is both hard wearing and crease resistant.

3 EQUIPMENT

Working with the correct tools rather than having to make do will make sewing far more pleasurable; it will also give a much more professional look to your cushions and covers. It is a long-term investment, so always buy the best tools you can afford and keep them in tiptop condition.

SEWING TOOLS

Storage of your hand-sewing tools is very important – there is nothing more frustrating than not being able to find things when you need them. A wooden box with a lid or a deep-sided plastic tray with a handle is ideal. Avoid using a cloth bag as scissors are liable to tear it.

A sewing machine is essential for soft furnishings. Projects such as loose covers or 'throws' involve a great many seams and these are best completed on a machine. Working on a machine is far quicker than by hand and the stitches are much stronger. The most important thing to remember when you are buying a sewing machine is that you know exactly how it operates, so if you are buying an electric sewing machine and you are offered a course of lessons do take advantage of them. Many people feel more confident with a simple electric machine that offers a straight and zig-zag stitch and has a free-arm, which is very useful for tackling awkward corners. If you think you are unlikely to use the variety of embroidery stitches and gadgets provided with a very expensive machine, then opt for a more basic model. Before stitching your fabric always test that the tension on the machine is correct by working on a remnant.

Needles should be stored in a cloth book or tin. You will need a variety of needles, including a bodkin for threading cords and elastic through casings. An upholstery needle is also very useful. Its curved shape makes it ideal for sewing cushions or making repairs.

Pins A box of these is essential; steel ones are best as they are less likely to mark fabric. Glass-headed pins are easier to identify in thick fabrics but they are extremely sharp and need to be handled with care. A pin cushion attached to your wrist is useful if you need to make alterations to a loose cover and need pins quickly.

Threads are available in a wide choice and you need to match up the correct type to the fabric you are working with. All basting should be completed with tacking thread but, as this breaks easily, ordinary thread should be used for gathering. The range of synthetic threads should be used on synthetic fibres and cotton threads should be used on natural fibres. If you use cotton on a synthetic fabric it is liable to shrink and cause the seams to pucker slightly.

Scissors need to be razor sharp for sewing or they will damage the cloth when you are cutting it out, causing it to snag. An old pair of scissors should be kept for cutting out paper patterns and a large pair of dressmaking shears reserved for cutting out fabric only. Embroidery scissors are ideal for small areas of work, cutting threads and to remove tacking stitches. Alternatively, you can buy a stitch ripper, which is a plastic rod with a pointed metal end that efficiently removes tacking and machine stitches. Pinking shears are also useful for soft furnishing as a way of trimming seams. Never be tempted to cut out your fabric with pinking shears, reserve these for trimming.

Tape measure This is a necessary part of your equipment. Choose one made of linen or fibreglass rather than stiffened paper so that it will not tear easily. A wooden ruler is also very useful, especially for measuring out quantities of fabric.

Dressmaker's squared paper is much easier to work with than plain paper if you are making your own patterns. You will only need a small quantity of squared paper if you are making and designing a cushion or trimming. Always mark your patterns clearly and store them in a labelled envelope so that the patterns can then be re-used.

French chalk, also known as tailor's chalk, is necessary for marking lines and instructions on cloth. Never be tempted to use biro or felt tip as both are difficult to remove. French chalk can be removed with a stiff brush. It can also be bought in the form of a pencil with a brush at one end.

A thimble is necessary when working with soft furnishing fabrics because you are liable to sew with heavier weight fabrics than in dressmaking. For this reason it is easier to work with a thimble, preferably a metal rather than a plastic one, worn on the middle finger.

PRESSING EQUIPMENT

Pressing is just as important as sewing. A perfectly flat seam or pleated edging add the final touch to a soft furnishing design. Ideally, you should have an iron and ironing board permanently set up in a spare room to save time. If you haven't sufficient space then try to store your ironing equipment close to your machine. It is a good rule to always have an ironing board set up whenever you are sewing.

Steam irons are especially useful for bulky fabrics. Keep the base of the iron clean and always empty a steam iron after use. Always test the iron on a remnant to ensure that no rusty stains are likely to mark your fabric.

Sleeve board This is useful for pressing into smaller more awkward corners.

A pressing mitt is ideal for darts or perhaps a cushion corner. It can be used by attaching it onto the narrower end of your sleeve board. On fabrics other than cottons and linens it is advisable to work with a pressing cloth made from muslin, cheesecloth or fine cotton.

A fine mist spray bottle can be used in conjunction with a dry iron, or to dampen areas when using a steam iron.

4 SEWING TECHNIQUES

BASIC HAND-SEWING STITCHES

Although the major part of sewing home furnishings is performed on a sewing machine certain steps need to be completed by hand.

Tacking, sometimes referred to as basting, is considered only as a temporary stitch for holding two pieces of fabric in place. Once you are an accomplished sewer it is possible to dispense with the tacking stage. Tacking stitches can be worked either with long equal stitches of about 1.5 cm (½ in) each or two stitches of 1.5 cm (½ in) each and one 2.5 cm (1 in) long. Tacking is used as a guide to provide a straight seam for machining and should be worked from right to left.

Running stitch is a smaller neater version of tacking and is used essentially for gathering an area of cloth. To ensure neat even gathers the stitches should be of equal length.

Back stitch is a strong stitch and is performed by working from left to right. It causes a continuous line of stitches on the right side of the fabric and overlapped stitches on the wrong side. Working from right to left bring the needle through from the back of the material about 3 mm (⅛ in) forward along the seam, then re-insert the needle this time about 3 mm (⅛ in) behind the point where the thread came through and bring it out 3 mm (⅛ in) forward on the seam line. As back stitch is such a strong stitch it can be used on seams where it is difficult to manoeuvre the machine.

Slip stitch is used for joining edges of fabric together such as on a mitred corner. Bring the needle through under the folded edge of the fabric, slide the needle along for about 5 mm (¼ in) and then put the needle into the other fold and draw up the thread. This stitch needs to be worked rather loosely.

Blanket stitch is often used for decorative purposes such as on the perimeter of a woollen throwover cover or blanket. It is worked on the right side of the cloth, stitching from left to right. Insert the needle at a right angle to the fabric, take the thread and, once the needle is pushed halfway out of the cloth, wind the thread under the needle. Then pull the needle the remainder of the way out of the cloth.

Overcasting is a stitch used to prevent edges of a cloth from fraying. Working from left to right, bring the needle through at an angle to the cloth, drawing the thread over the edge of the cloth.

Hemming is worked on the wrong side of the fabric and from right to left. Insert the needle a little way under the folded edge picking up a thread of fabric, take the needle into the hem and push it out. Do not pull the thread too tightly or the seam will pucker.

MACHINE-STITCHED SEAMS

Before stitching with your machine it is important to test that the tension is correct. Work a few rows of stitching on a spare piece of cloth rather than on your cushion or loose cover.

When sewing a **plain or open seam,** work with the right sides of the fabric facing each other, then pin and tack the edges together. Tacking stitches need to be worked about 1.5 mm (½ in) inside the actual machine line, in case they are liable to mark it. Stitch the seam and make sure both ends of the stitching are quite secure. Remove the tacking stitches. Press the seam open, pressing on the wrong side of the cloth. To strengthen the seams you may wish to neaten the edges.

A french seam is a particularly strong seam, generally used on lighter-weight fabrics, and suitable for cushion covers, pillow cases or bed covers. Take the two pieces of fabric, with *wrong* sides together, and make a seam about 5 mm (¼ in) from the edge. Carefully trim the seam close to the stitching and turn it through so that the right sides are now facing. Work another row of stitching to enclose the raw edges of the material.

A flat fell seam is another strong seam but better suited to firmer heavier fabrics. When using this seam, bear in mind that the stitching is visible on the right side of the fabric. Position the *wrong* sides of the fabric together and machine 1.5 cm (½ in) from the edge. Press the seam open and then carefully trim one side of the seam only close to the machining. Take the other seam edge (the one that has not been trimmed) and fold it over the trimmed one then machine it close to the fold.

Seam finishes
To both strengthen and neaten seams, any of the following methods can be used. The quickest and easiest way to finish a seam is by using pinking shears. Once the seam has been pressed open simply trim the seam edges with the shears. Remember this method is not ideal for fabrics that fray easily. Another method is to work machine zig-zag stitches along the seam edges. Seams can also be finished by turning the seam edge under and stitching it in place.

MACHINE-STITCHED HEMS

Unlike dressmaking most soft furnishing designs need to be finished by machined hems. A hand-sewn hem is rarely strong enough to cope with the hard wear that cushions and covers have to withstand. To make a double hem, take your raw edge and make a narrow turning to the inside of 5 mm (¼ in), then press this turning in place. Turn the fabric over again to the depth of hem you require and press the hem again. Machine stitch the hem in place close to the folded edge. On thick woollen fabrics, felt and other cloths that are not liable to fray, simply pink the raw edge then turn the cloth up to the length you require, machining close to the pinked edge to finish.

For a less bulky finish use the zig-zag on your machine and make two rows of machining over the raw edge. Turn the fabric to the inside, to the length you require, and machine the hem in place stitching close to the neatened raw edge.

Mastering the various techniques involved in constructing a cushion or loose cover can give your design a really professional finish, but it is techniques such as frills, piping and pleats that can turn a very simple design into something far more decorative and interesting.

Cot bumpers, scatter cushions and dressing table cover all in matching fabric create a startling effect in this child's room

PIPING

Piping is essentially used to emphasize the outline of a piece of furniture or covering. It can either be made in co-ordinating fabric or in a contrasting colour for a more dramatic effect. Piping can add extra strength to covers on areas that might receive constant hard wear, such as around the arms and the cushions on a sofa.

Preparing piping

Piping is prepared by covering cord or twine with strips of fabric cut on the bias. The bias strip has some stretch and can be shaped round curves. To find the true bias of a piece of cloth, fold it diagonally so that a straight edge (or horizontal grain) is parallel to the vertical grain. Press the fabric on the diagonal fold, open it out and use the crease as a guide to mark parallel lines the desired width of the strip plus 1.5 cm (½ in) for seams (fig. 2). Most cord available today should be pre-shrunk. If you are unsure it is best to wash the cord and dry it thoroughly before using it for your cushions or covers.

Once you have cut strips of bias fabric you will then need to join them together. Take the ends of two strips and place them right sides together making sure that the two ends form an angle, like an arched shape, then stitch the ends together, making sure you leave a seam (fig. 3). Press the seam open, on both the right and wrong side of the cloth to ensure that it lays absolutely flat, and trim the ends.

With wrong sides of the fabric together fold the bias strip in half and lightly press. Open out the strip, place the length of cord onto the pressed line, then close the strip with the cord inside. The strip is now ready to be machined (fig. 4). To make sewing easier it is advisable to work with a zip foot to enable the stitching to sit closely to the covered cord. If you find handling the piping strip rather awkward, first

2 *Making the piping: cut strips along crossway fold making them wide enough to cover the cord plus 1.5 cm (½ in) for seams*

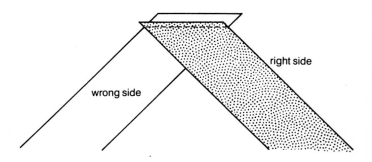

3 *Join the bias strips, stitching the ends together in an arched shape*

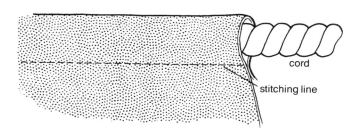

4 *Insert cord in piping, and then stitch close to the cord*

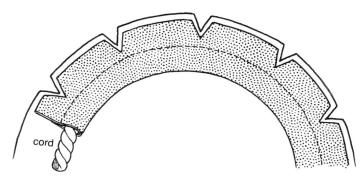

5 *Slash bias strip before adding cord for fitting on a curved edge*

pin then tack the cord into place, remembering to remove the tacking once the machining has been completed.

Joining the piping to the fabric
Having made the piping it needs to be carefully joined to the main fabric to ensure that it lays quite smoothly in place. When attaching piping to your work always begin on a straight edge rather than a curved one. Once you are proficient at working with piping it will be possible for the cord and its casing to be pinned with the fabric and sewn in one operation. However, if you are inexperienced always make the piping carefully first, then attach it to the fabric with a second set of machining.

Take your length of piping and pin it to your fabric, pinning it to the right side of the cloth. Keep the raw edges even, then machine the pieces together. Take the second piece of fabric, and, with right sides together, place it over the piping so that the piping is now sandwiched between the two pieces of fabric. Make a second row of machining. Remove any pins or tacking stitches and turn the work through to the right side. When you come to a corner you will need to make a cut about 1 cm (3⁄8 in) in from the corner edge to allow for ease,

and, as a precaution, make one or two back stitches inside the seam at the corner for added strength. If your work involves a continuous curved edge, such as a round cushion, you need to slash the bias strip at regular intervals of 3 cm (1 1⁄8 in), before wrapping it around the cord (fig. 5). Creating this extra ease in the strip will ensure that it moulds itself to the very shape you require.

Joining cord edges
Firstly trim off any excess strands of yarn and neaten the ends so that they are even. Position the two cord ends together, then bind them with matching sewing thread (fig. 6). Bind as neatly and smoothly as possible to avoid a lumpy finish

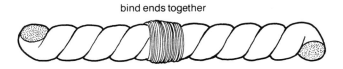

6 *Joining edges of cord together: butt the two ends of the cord and bind with matching thread*

showing through the piping. To join the fabric pieces, make narrow turnings to neaten on one edge, lay the other edge inside the neatened one and machine them together.

A continuous strip of bias fabric for use on a larger project such as piping around the edge of a throwover cover, or on a sofa, can be made in the following way. Take your strip of fabric and fold the right hand corner to the top edge, to obtain the true bias. Make a thumb crease to mark the fold line, then unfold the fabric. Cut along the crease line and then attach this triangle to the other end of the strip with the freshly-cut edge facing outwards (fig. 7). Stitch the triangle in place, press the seam and trim it. Mark off your bias strips on the fabric, using french chalk and working on the wrong side of the cloth. Take the top edge of the strip and with right sides together, fold it over, positioning the right hand top corner edge to meet the second bias line marked on your fabric, not the first. Pin along the seam, making sure that the lines match up exactly, then tack and seam the fabric. This will form a tube. (When cutting the fabric to make the continuous strip, this will create a spiral effect.) Starting at the right hand end of the tube and working with small

scissors, cut along the chalk lines to make your continuous strip of binding.

FRILLS

Frills bring a softening effect to any room. They are highly decorative and can instantly create an informal atmosphere.

In order for frills to hang correctly they should be cut from the width of the fabric, with the selvedge running down the depth of the strip. Decide on the width of the frill you need then add the seam allowances. If you are using a single frill, firstly neaten one edge of the strip by turning under the raw edge and machining it in place. On more delicate fabrics you may wish to hand-sew the hem as it will be visible. For a double frill calculate the finished width you require, double this and add the seam allowances. Fold the strip in half lengthways with wrong sides together. Work a row of gathering threads, either by hand or using the largest stitch on your machine inside the seam allowance, stitching through both thicknesses of cloth (fig. 8).

Having made the first row of gathering stitches about 3 mm (⅛in) inside the seam allowance, make a second row 3 mm (⅛in) below the first. Draw up the thread ends to the length you require, adjust the level of fullness equally and pin the frill to your

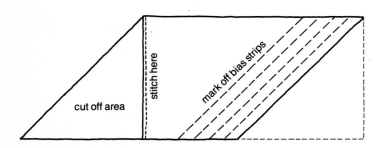

7 *Making piping for a larger project: attach cut-off triangle to other end of fabric*

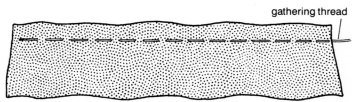

8 *A double frill: work gathering thread completed on the machine on inside of seam allowance*

This attractive but awkward-shaped seat has been made more comfortable with the addition of fabric-covered foam cushions

fabric making sure the thread ends have been securely tied. Allow a little extra fullness if your frill is on a corner.

PLEATS

To ensure that pleats have that really professional touch it is vitally important that they are spaced at equal distances apart. Pleats are most often found on the bottom edge of loose covers or throwovers for the bedroom.

Decide on the depth of pleat you need then add the seam allowance for the top edge and hem for the lower one. Hem the lower edge of the strip and then iron it quite firmly to eliminate any wrinkles. For box pleats cut a piece of stiff card to the width of pleat you require, for example 7 cm (2¾ in). With tailor's chalk mark the pleat every 8 cm (3 in), marking both the top and lower edge of the strip of fabric (fig. 9). Once the entire strip has been

marked fold it into pleats, first pinning then tacking them into position, leaving a small space between pleats (fig. 10). This should be done along the top and lower edge of the pleat to hold it securely in place. Having removed the pins, press the pleats firmly in place. Then machine along the top edge only. Remove the tacking and, with right sides together, pin the pleats to your fabric.

The size of pleats can be varied to suit your taste and you can experiment with different widths by using strips of paper before marking your fabric.

MITRING

Being able to make a neat corner and to keep it flat is a great asset in sewing home furnishings. It is a technique commonly known as mitring. This skill can be employed when making openings for loose covers or bed covers. Mitring is especially suitable for thick fabrics to help to eliminate bulk.

Take the piece of fabric to be folded and then make two fold lines, first one then the other of equal widths. It is essential that the turnings are equal or the corner will not be perfectly finished. Press both the turnings lightly to set the fold lines. Open the

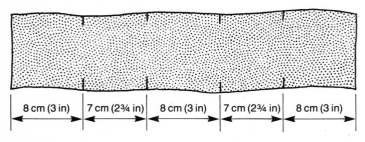

| 8 cm (3 in) | 7 cm (2¾ in) | 8 cm (3 in) | 7 cm (2¾ in) | 8 cm (3 in) |

9 *With tailor's chalk mark the pleat every 8 cm (3 in), marking both the top and lower edge of the fabric*

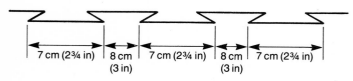

| 7 cm (2¾ in) | 8 cm (3 in) | 7 cm (2¾ in) | 8 cm (3 in) | 7 cm (2¾ in) |

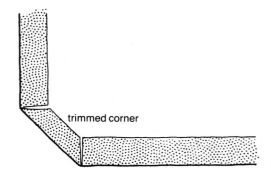

trimmed corner

10 *Fold the pleats into position then press firmly*

11 *Trim away the upper part of the corner to reduce bulk*

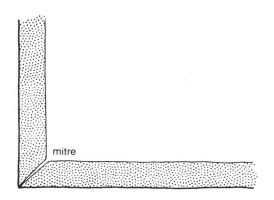

12 *Re-fold the original turnings to form the mitre*

piece of fabric out flat again and fold the corner in and trim away the upper part of the corner to reduce bulk (fig. 11). Now re-fold the original turnings along the crease lines to form the mitre (fig. 12). Hand-sew the folded edges together using a slip stitch and press lightly to re-define the edge.

SCALLOPED EDGES

This very attractive type of edging can be used to trim the corners of a throwover cover.

Like pleats, the success of a scalloped edge is determined by scallops being the same depth and an equal distance apart. Ideally it is best to make a paper pattern of your scalloped edge before transferring it on to fabric. Decide on the depth of your scallop which can be made by tracing around a small plate, saucer or cup and allow for your seam. Cut out the paper pattern and then pin it to your fabric and cut out the scalloped edge. The raw edge can be simply finished by machining around the raw curved edge with a small zig-zag stitch. You will need to do this twice in order to secure the raw edge effectively.

For a firmer finish, cut out two strips of fabric with a scalloped edge, one can be from lining fabric if you haven't sufficient furnishing fabric. With right sides together stitch the scalloped edges together, clipping into the corners (fig. 13) and trimming close to the stitching before turning the scallops through to the right side. Gently pull the scallops into shape and then press firmly before attaching the shaped edge to your main piece of work.

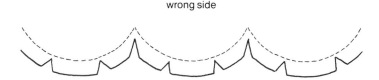

13 *Clipping into the edges of the scallops*

BOUND EDGES

Contrasting strips of bias binding can make an inexpensive yet colourful trim for cushions or 'throws'. You can either buy the binding ready-made or make your own from oddments of fabric. You might like to trim a throwover cover with a variety of different prints joined together. This would provide an eye-catching contrast to a plain cover.

If the binding is being sandwiched between two layers of fabric it can be applied in the same way as piping but omitting the cord. If binding is used to finish a single layer of fabric, first, stitch it to your fabric with right sides together. Bring the remaining longer edge to the wrong side of the fabric and, making a narrow turning, either machine or hand-sew in place. Join strips of bias binding following the method given in the piping section.

PART II

5 MAKING A BASIC CUSHION

You can either make a new cushion right from scratch, or you can simply cover an existing one in a new fabric. In either case the first cushion you choose to make should be a simple square. More complicated shapes are better left until you have gained confidence with a basic design.

THE INNER COVER
Having decided on the size of cushion you need, you will then need to measure for the inner cover. Sateen and calico are the most suitable coverings for all types of filling apart from down and feathers. Both of these should be covered with either downproof cambric or ticking.

To create an attractive plump appearance, cushions with loose fillings such as feathers, down, kapok, wadding and foam chips need to have an inner cover 1 cm (⅜ in) larger on all the seams than the outer cover. Solid fillings such as foam, and their inner covers, need to be made to exactly the same size as the cushion cover. Inner covers need to be kept as smooth and neat as possible, particularly if the cushion cover is in a lightweight cloth. Any unsightly bumps or ridges from the filling will be visible from the outside of the cushion and will make the resulting cushion look home-made.

Having marked out the size of your inner cover plus 1.5 cm (½ in) seam allowances, cut two pieces of cloth. With right sides together, pin, tack and then machine the seams leaving one edge free. Stitch along both remaining ends of the free edge for just 3 cm (1⅛ in). Make a second row of stitching just inside the seam allowance for added strength. Secure the stitches either end of the opening. Trim the corners and pink the seams and turn the cover to the right side (fig. 14). Push out all the corners with the end of a knitting needle and press the cushion to remove creases.

Insert the filling and ensure that the pad feels quite firm. Keeping edges in line with the seam, close the opening with a neat even slip stitch in a toning thread.

THE CUSHION COVER
Taking a sheet of dressmaker's squared paper, draw out your cushion pattern, allowing 1.5 cm (½ in) for seams. Cut out the pattern and place it on your fabric, reserving the selvedge for the opening if possible. In this way you will avoid having to neaten the raw edge for the opening. For patterned cloth you will need more material than for plain cloth, so that you can cut each cover piece separately so that any attractive motif can be positioned in the centre of the cushion.

With right sides together, pin and then tack the edges together. If you feel proficient enough to

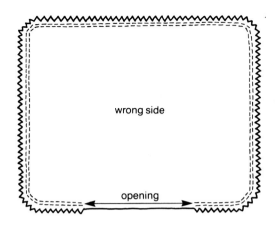

wrong side

opening

14 *Making the inner cover: pink the seams and trim the corners, and turn the cover to the right side*

avoid the tacking stage, insert your pins at right angles to the fabric edge and your sewing machine should stitch over the pins without you having to remove them first. This will ensure that you have an even line of stitching, which is harder to achieve when removing pins. Stitch around three edges of the cushion, leaving the opening edge free. Stitch for 3 cm (1⅛ in) along both remaining ends (in the same way as the inner cover).

Trim the corners and trim the seam allowances to 1 cm (⅜ in), then zig-zag the seam edges to neaten and strengthen them.

OPENINGS AND FASTENINGS

A sufficiently wide opening is one of the most important points to consider when sewing a cushion. As you will want to be able to remove the inner cover easily it is necessary for almost one complete side of the cover to be reserved for the opening.

Slip stitch fastening

One of the simplest methods of fastening a cushion cover is to use a hand-sewn slip stitch. First, neaten the raw edges of the opening either with the zig-zag stitch on your machine or making a narrow hem and machining it in place. If you have used the selvedges for the opening the fabric edges will not need to be neatened.

Insert the filling into the cushion cover and then slip stitch the opening to close it. Work with thread that matches the colour of the cushion and keep the stitches small and even, keeping the edges in line with the seam. This type of fastening is suitable for decorative cushions in lightweight fabrics only. It is not particularly strong and if the cushion receives plenty of hard wear and needs frequent washing, constantly unpicking the stitching will prove very tiresome.

Press fasteners

These are mainly suitable for decorative cushions that will not receive too much hard wear or the fasteners are likely to pop open. They are suitable for lightweight fabrics but are more convenient than using a slip stitch. To provide a firm backing for the fasteners make a double hem on the opening seams by turning the fabric under once, then again, and then machining it in place.

Fastening tape

Press studs can be purchased on a canvas strip and sewn into place by stitching down either side of the strip. As the strips are about 2.5 cm (1 in) wide you will need to make a flap for the opening edge. To do this take your paper pattern and add 3 cm (1⅛ in) to the opening area only. Make up the cushion in the usual way. Make a narrow hem on the flap edge and then machine the fastening tape in place turning the ends under to prevent them fraying.

Velcro touch-and-close spots and strips

Velcro can be purchased in strips and machined in place in the same way as the fastening tape or it can be hand-sewn in place by using small Velcro spots. Velcro is made from two tapes with different surfaces, one has small nylon hooks, the other has a coarse brush-like surface. The two surfaces 'lock' together when pressed firmly. Velcro is suitable for most types of fastening but is not ideal for sheer fabrics. It is worth noting that Velcro spots and strips should be fastened before being put in the washing machine or the hooks are liable to snag other fabrics. As Velcro is 2 cm (¾ in) wide it will be necessary to add a flap to your cushion opening as described for the fastening tape. Strips should be machined in place and spots can be secured with tiny back stitches worked in the shape of a square.

Zip fasteners

Zips are perhaps the most widely used type of fastening. They are neat and strong and you can generally colour-match them to your fabric. As zips can be slightly awkward to sew into a seam you may prefer to finish your opening edge before stitching the remaining seams. The zip will need to be 6 cm (2⅜ in) shorter than the entire length of the opening edge. Where possible try to position the zip on a straight edge of your cushion. For greater ease you may prefer to stitch the zip in place using a small back stitch.

With right sides together pin, tack and then machine along the opening ends for 3 cm (1⅛ in). Then tack the remaining opening edges together along the seam line. With the wrong side of the fabric uppermost, position the zip in place. Tack, then machine the zip in place, making a double row of stitching at the top edges and base of the zip to strengthen it. Remove the tacking and then proceed to stitch the remaining edges of the cushion.

If you have a cushion with an embroidered or appliquéd front and a plain back you may prefer to attach your zip to the back to avoid any strain being placed on the edge of the work. Take your pattern piece and cut it in half then add an extra 1.5 cm (½ in) to the centre back edge. Insert the zip as you would for a side opening but working on the centre back seam of the cushion.

Back vent opening

This type of opening is mainly suitable for decorative cushions in lightweight fabrics only. It provides a quick and easy finish and enables the

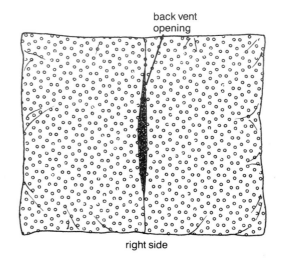

15 *Back vent opening: leave open to insert filling*

inner cover to be removed easily. Cut out the front cover piece, then cut out the back piece twice. Neaten the centre back edge of each back piece by making a double hem and machining or hand-sewing it in place. With right sides together stitch a back piece to either side of the front piece. Overlap the back pieces so that they line up with the front then stitch down the vent for just 5 cm (2 in), and complete stitching the remaining side seams. Turn to the right side and insert the filling (fig. 15). The two halves of the back will lie together as if closed without further fastening, and the inner filling is easy to remove when necessary.

Fastenings as a feature

For most projects it is likely that you will want to disguise the opening area as much as possible. However, you may wish to design your cushion so that the fastening becomes a feature of the cushion.

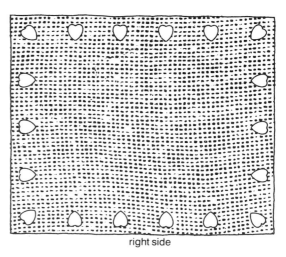

17 *Using novelty buttons to fasten edges together*

Snap-on fasteners are colourful easy-to-apply studs which would make a colourful finish to a cushion for a teenager's room. Take your two cushion cover pieces and, instead of stitching them together, make a double hem and mitre the corners. Press the cushion edges firmly. With wrong sides together position the front and back pieces together and secure around all the edges with snap-on fasteners (fig. 16).

Button fastenings are easy to make and look very attractive. Neaten your two cushion covers as described for the snap-on fasteners. Then sew pretty-coloured buttons to the wrong side of the back cushion edges and corresponding buttonholes on the front edges. Insert the inner cushion and button the edges to finish (fig. 17).

Ribbon is an alternative to buttons and gives a more delicate finish on lace and silk fabrics. Sew lengths of ribbon at 4 cm (1½ in) intervals on the front and back pieces to hold them together and tie

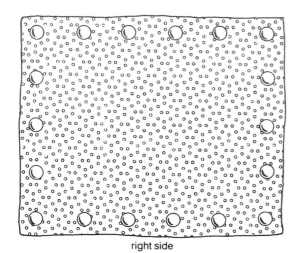

16 *Using snap-on fasteners to secure the edges of your cushion pieces together*

The floral design on this cushion is echoed in a stencil motif which carries right round the walls, door and onto the furniture

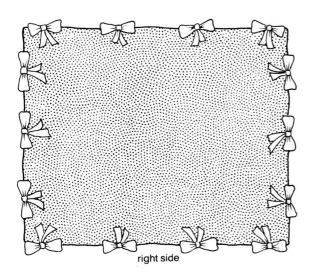

right side

18 *Alternatively, the edges can be tied together with lengths of ribbon*

with decorative bows (fig. 18). If you are working with a brightly-coloured print you may like to use a variety of different coloured ribbons and on firmer heavier fabrics use coloured braid instead of ribbon.

Alternatively, punch eyelet holes through the fabric at regular intervals making sure they correspond on the front and back cushion edges, then thread ribbon through the holes and tie it at one corner.

6 ALTERNATIVE SHAPES FOR CUSHIONS

No matter how proficient you may be about making soft furnishings, it is wise to make a paper pattern for everything. Proportions can easily be rectified on paper, but it is impossible to re-shape fabric once it has been cut.

ROUND CUSHIONS

Round cushions need to be made from a perfect circle. If you are making a small cushion you may have some household utensil available that you can draw round, perhaps the rim of a large mixing bowl or saucepan. However, if you are drawing a circle free-hand always work with dressmaker's squared paper. First, measure out a square of paper roughly to the size of cushion you require. Fold the paper in half and then half again. Using a rounded object such as a saucer or plate, trace a curve from one corner of the folded paper to the other, then cut along the curved line (fig. 19). Open out the paper and you have a circle. You will need to add 1.5 cm (½ in) round the edge for your seam allowance.

You can choose to position your opening on a round cushion in the seam, but it is easier to have an opening in the back piece, especially if you are inserting a zip. Take the pattern and slash it in half widthways. Make an allowance for 1.5 cm (½ in) on all edges for seams and insert the zip before joining the front and back pieces together.

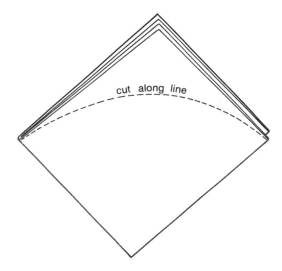

cut along line

19 *To create a circle, fold a square piece of paper in half, and then in half again, and trace a curve from one corner to the other*

TRIANGULAR AND HEART-SHAPED CUSHIONS

Measure out a square of paper roughly to the size you require. Fold the paper in half and measure out half of your triangle or heart, then cut the pattern out omitting to cut along the folded edge. An opening for a triangular-shaped cushion is sewn into the base. For a heart-shaped cushion the zip is sewn into the back piece one quarter of the way down from the top of the heart.

BORDER CUSHIONS

Moving one step on from a basic square cushion are border cushions. This type of cushion requires no piped or frilled edge because the decorative edging is cut in one with the cushion piece. The variations on this type of design mean that you can choose to have a single or double border.

Single border cushions

To make your pattern, measure out the size of cushion you need, add to this amount an extra 6 cm (2⅜ in) for your border (you can make the border wider if you wish) plus your seam allowance. Cut out your paper pattern to these dimensions, then place the pattern on your fabric and cut out the front piece. Slash the pattern in half and add an

extra 1.5 cm (½ in) for the centre back seam then cut out two pieces for the back. With right sides together stitch the centre back seam leaving an opening for a zip, then insert the zip (fig. 20). With right sides together stitch the cushion pieces together. Turn the cover through to the right side and press. Measure and mark, using tailor's chalk, your stitching lines on the right side of the cover 6 cm (2⅜ in) from the outside edge. Stitch over the chalk lines again.

Double border cushions

To make your pattern, measure out the size of cushion you need, add to this an extra 12 cm (4¾ in) for your border (this will give a finished

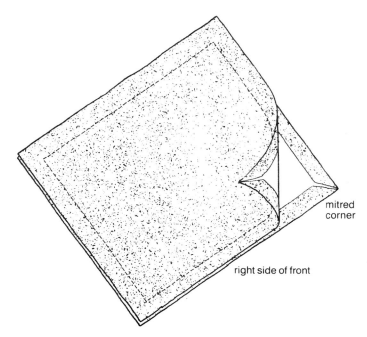

zip opening

right side of back

20 *Insert zip into back seam*

mitred corner

right side of front

21 *Stitch cover pieces together*

border width of 6 cm (2⅜ in)), plus your seam allowance. Cut out your paper pattern to these dimensions, then place the pattern on your fabric and cut out the front piece. Make up the back piece and put in a zip for the opening, as described for a single border cushion. Make a 6 cm (2⅜ in) turning, plus seam allowance, to the wrong side of the fabric on all the raw edges of the cushion. Press under the turnings and mitre the corners (fig. 21). Measure and mark, using tailor's chalk, your stitching line on the right side of the front piece. Pin the two cushion pieces together, wrong sides facing, and stitch over the chalk lines.

PIPED CUSHIONS

Piped cushions are one of the most popular types of cushion. Once you have made a simple square-shaped cushion you need only add a length of piping for a really professional finish. You can choose to work your piping in co-ordinating or contrasting fabric. For a first attempt it would be advisable to work with co-ordinating fabric to disguise less-than-perfect seams.

Begin by taking your cushion pattern and, allowing for your seams, measure round the outside edge. To this figure add another 10 cm (4 in) for ease and joining the ends of the piping. Your strip of bias-cut fabric and cord should be cut to this length. You can choose to pipe your cushion with a thick wide cord or a narrow one. Narrow cord is suitable for lightweight fabrics, a medium cord is ideal for firmer fabrics such as linens and cottons and a wide cord is usually reserved for loose covers.

Take the front piece of your cushion cover and start to pin the cord around the edges on the right side of the fabric. It is best to join cord away from a corner and not near an opening. Ease the cord

carefully at the corners snipping into the bias strip so that it sits neatly at the edges. Having pinned the cord in place then tack it. Butt the ends of the cord together and secure following the method given on page 25.

Replace the foot on your machine with a zip foot, then stitch the piping in place (fig. 22). With right sides together pin then tack the back piece of your cushion cover in place, then machine it leaving the opening edge free. Complete the fastening using one of the methods given. A zip fastener or a hand-sewn slip stitched finish are the most common types of fastening for a piped cushion as they avoid extra bulk. A piped round cushion is prepared in the same way as the square one but the strip of bias fabric that encloses the cord should be snipped at 3 cm (1⅛ in) intervals so that the piping moulds itself to the shape of the cushion.

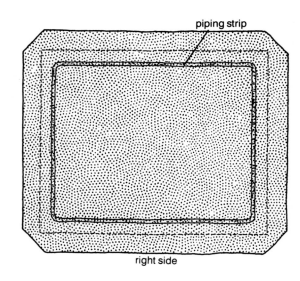

22 *Stitch piping to the right side of the front cushion piece, keeping all raw edges even*

Two contrasting fabrics are used with dazzling effect in this room. Behind them is draped a Paisley patterned throwover

If you feel rather nervous about using a piped edging you can create a similar effect by adding colourful cord and hand-sewing it in place. Make up your square or round cushion in the usual way. Measure round the finished edge of the cushion and allow 10 cm (4 in) for ease and securing the ends and buy some attractive cord or braiding to this length. Position the cord on the cushion seams, tack it in place, then hand-sew it in place stitching both sides of the cord into position to the front and back of the cushion cover. For a more decorative finish begin and end sewing your cord at one corner and make a tassel by unwinding the cord end and then re-tying a knot.

FRILLED CUSHIONS

Plain frill

A frilled edge makes a very attractive finish to a simple round or square cushion. However, you will need to allow for extra cloth depending on the width of your frill.

For a single frill take your paper pattern and, allowing for seams, measure the outside edge. Double this measurement and cut a strip of fabric to this length plus 3 cm (1⅛ in) seam allowance for joining the strip. Neaten one raw edge by making a double hem and machining it in place. Then join the strip of fabric to make a circle, trim the seam and press it flat. Run a gathering thread around the remaining raw edge. Take your front cushion cover piece and, with right sides together, draw up the gathering thread so that the frill fits the circumference of the cushion (fig. 23), allowing slightly more gathers at the corners on a square cushion. Pin, tack and then machine the gathers in position. On a large cushion it is easier to divide the

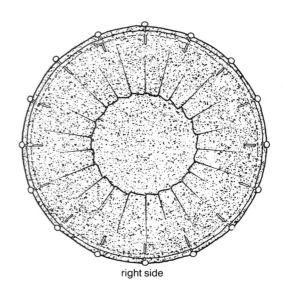

right side

23 *Fixing a frill to a round cushion: ease gathers to fit front cushion piece, then pin in place*

frill into four sections before pulling up the gathers, then pin each section to a side of the cushion. For a round cushion mark the cushion into quarters before pinning the frill in place. On firmer fabrics where the thread may break it is advisable to work two rows of gathering thread.

Take the back cushion cover piece and place it over the front one, with all edges even, stitch the frill in place leaving the opening area free.

For a double frill, take the measurement for the single frill for the length. Calculate the width of frill you need then double it. With right sides together join the ends of your frill, trim and press the seam. Then fold the strip in half with wrong sides together and lightly press the fold line. Work a gathering thread along the raw edges and attach to the cushion as described for a single frill.

Pleated frill

A pleated frill creates a slightly more formal image than a plain one. A pleated frill is time consuming so allow for this as all the pleats need to be made an equal size. To calculate the amount of fabric you need, first measure the outside edge of your cushion. Decide on the width of your pleat and multiply this by the total measurement of the outside edge, allow an extra two pleats for each corner and a seam allowance where the ends will be joined. Cut out your strip of fabric, neaten one raw edge, pin your pleats into position, then tack them and press firmly in place. Join the strip to form a circle and, with right sides together, pin it to the front cushion cover piece. Overlap the pleats at the corners, then machine the pleats in place.

Frilled and piped cushions

Taking your front cushion cover piece, attach the piping in place and then stitch the frill in position over the piping, before adding the back cushion cover piece.

BOLSTER CUSHIONS

These round sausage-shaped cushions have been traditionally used to support pillows on a bed. Bolsters can also be used as a means of support on an open-ended sofa. A bolster pad can be bought ready-made.

If you want to make your own bolster, use calico or sateen fabric and fill with polystyrene granules. To make your pattern, decide on the length of your bolster and the depth. Draw out the main piece of the cushion and then draw the circle for the ends. Cut the main piece once and the circle twice. With right sides together stitch the main piece to form a tube leaving a small opening to insert the granules.

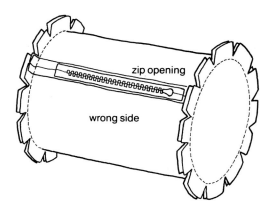

24 *Making a bolster cushion. Add the end pieces to the bolster snipping in at the seam allowance for ease*

Attach the circles to each end, snipping in at the seam allowance to allow for ease. Turn the cover through to the right side, insert the filling and slip stitch the opening to close it.

Place your pattern on your fabric and cut out as for the inner cover, and adding 1.5 cm ($\frac{1}{2}$ in) seam allowance. Using a zip 6 cm ($2\frac{3}{8}$ in) shorter than the length of the bolster, insert it in position. Stitch the seam either end of the zip to complete the tube. Stitch the end pieces to the bolster, snipping in at the seam allowance to allow for ease (fig. 24). Turn the bolster through to the right side, insert the filling pad and close the zip.

Gathered bolster cushions

This type of cushion is used for decorative purposes and, as the gathered end is likely to be hidden underneath pillows, it is used mainly on sofas.

Take your paper pattern for the main part of your bolster cushion and add 3 cm ($1\frac{1}{8}$ in) to each end. Cut out one piece of fabric to this size. Insert the zip as described previously and finish the seam. Neaten the ends of the tube with a double hem. Then stitch a gathering thread close to the folded edge. Gently draw up the gathering threads at each end so that the edges of the fabric meet. Position a covered button or tassel at each end of the bolster enclosing the gathered ends and stitch them firmly in position. Insert the filling and close the zip to finish.

Instead of gathering the ends of your bolster you may like to extend the main part for a further 7 cm (2¾ in) each end, neaten the ends and tie them with a pretty ribbon or cord into a cracker shape. This type of finish is ideal for decorative cushions and not for those liable to receive hard wear.

BOX CUSHIONS

Cushions of this kind have a welt running around the circumference creating a box effect. The cushion can either be square or round. Box cushions are most often filled with a foam pad that has been cut to the exact size of the cushion. To enable the foam filling to be removed easily a zip is positioned in the welt and, unlike the simple square cushion, the zip continues around the adjoining two corners for 6 cm (2⅜ in).

Square box cushions

Using squared paper calculate the length and width of your cushion and draw out your pattern. Decide on the depth of your welt and make it long enough to equal the circumference of your cushion. To create a more structured finish cut your welt strip into four pieces following the diagram. Then slash the piece where the opening is to go in half (fig. 25). Position your pattern pieces on your fabric and cut out allowing for all seams. Stitch the zip in place following the method given for a square cushion.

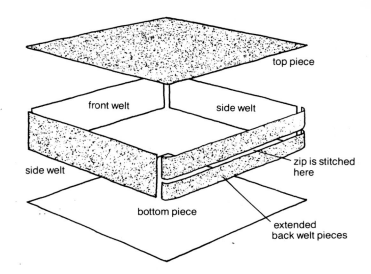

25 *The pieces which make up a square box cushion*

With right sides together join the remaining welt pieces together to form a strip. With right sides together attach the bottom cushion piece in place, clipping the seam allowance of the welt and trimming the corners to allow for ease. Then with right sides together stitch the top cushion piece in place, again trimming corners and clipping the seam allowance. Turn the cushion right side out, gently pushing the corners out, insert the filling and close the zip to finish.

Round box cushions

These are made in the same way as the square cushions, however the welt is made from two not four strips joined together. One strip houses the zip, which is half the circumference of the cushion.

Cut out your paper pattern for the top and bottom pieces plus the welt pieces. Slash the welt piece that houses the zip in half lengthways and

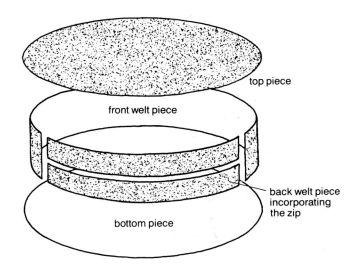

26 *The pieces which make up a round box cushion*

insert the zip (fig. 26). With right sides together join the two welt pieces together to form a circle. With right sides together join the welt to the bottom piece of the round cushion. Snip at 3 cm (1⅛ in) intervals into the seam allowance to allow for ease, repeat this with the top piece. Insert the filling and close the zip to finish.

SQUAB CUSHIONS

This type of cushion is designed to be cut to the exact shape of the chair seat, ties are then attached to the cushion to secure it in position. The opening is most often put across the back piece.

Taking your squared paper lay it over the seat of your chair and trace around the exact shape of the top. Mark the position of the arms and legs so that you know where to attach the ties.

Place your pattern on your fabric and, allowing for seams, cut out a front piece. Slash the pattern in half widthways, position the two pieces on your fabric and cut them out allowing for seams on all the edges.

Insert the zip into the centre back seam. Cut strips of bias binding, ribbon or narrow tubes of matching fabric and pin them to the back piece over the markings. The ties should be long enough to tie in a bow. They should be folded in half and the folded edge pinned to the seam allowance of the cushion.

With right sides together position the front and back cushion pieces together and stitch incorporating the ties. Turn through to the right side, insert the filling and close the zip to finish (fig. 27).

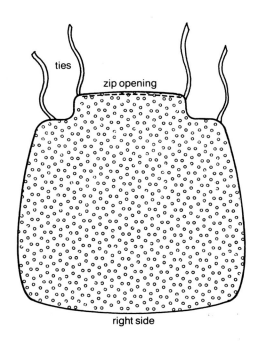

27 *A squab cushion: the cushion is made to the exact shape of the chair*

Piping on squab, box and bolster cushions

Piping can be used on squab, bolster and box cushions. You will need to measure the circumference of the cushion once for a squab cushion. For a box cushion measure the circumference and double the amount as the piping will need to be sewn with the top and lower edge of the welt. Both ends of the bolster cushion can be piped before stitching the round ends in position.

Fillings for squab and box cushions

Both squab and box cushions are best filled with a piece of foam cut to exactly the same shape and size as the cushion cover. As both types of cushion demand a smooth finish an inner cover is not necessary.

PILLOW CASES

Making a pillow case is an ideal project for a beginner as it requires no fastenings. Pillow cases can be made from soft silky fabrics or easy-care cottons.

Using squared paper draw out the size of your pillow case measuring around your pillow as a guide. Cut out your front pillow piece, allowing for seams. Add an extra 18 cm (7 in) to the length of your back pillow piece for the tuck-in flap. Cut the pillow out allowing for seams. Neaten the shorter end of the flap and one shorter end of the front piece with a double hem. With right sides together pin the front to the back bringing the flap over to sit on the front piece. Stitch the side seams and zig-zag stitch to neaten. Turn the pillow case to the right side pushing out the corners and press to finish.

Pillow cases with frilled edging

Cut out a frilled edge to fit your pillow case. With right sides together pin it to the front section only. Tack, then machine the frill in place easing the gathers evenly around the sides. Cut the back and flap pieces separately this time, adding a 1.5 cm (½ in) seam allowance to the cut edges. Neaten one long edge of the flap piece. Position the flap piece on the front piece with right sides together and the frill between them, stitch along the remaining longer edge. Turn through to the right side. Take the back piece and neaten one short edge. With right sides together pin the front and back pieces together then stitch around the edges, leaving the opening area with the flap free (fig. 28).

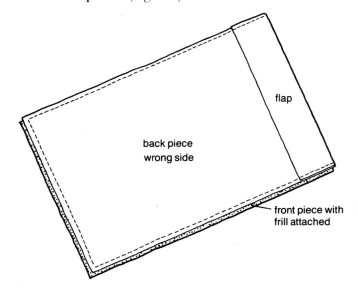

back piece
wrong side

flap

front piece with
frill attached

28 *Pillow case with frill: stitch front and back together, incorporating the flap*

7   DECORATING CUSHIONS

Using piping and adding frills are attractive ways of trimming cushions, but there are also many other techniques that you could experiment with.

RIBBONS AND BRAIDS

Ribbons and braids make an easy-to-apply decoration to a cushion cover. Take your front cushion piece and pin ribbon or braid around the edges. Cut the ribbon into four pieces and mitre it at the corners for a professional finish (fig. 29). When you pin the ribbon in place, do so making an allowance for the seams. Tack the ribbon and then machine it in place, working two rows of stitching either side of the ribbon. On a plain-coloured cushion cover cut strips from a remnant of fabric as an alternative to ribbon. Cut the fabric into strips to the width you require, allowing for turnings. Press under a turning on the raw edges, mitring the corners. Tack, then machine the strips in place on a plain-coloured cushion cover.

If you have velvet curtains or suite, you can use strips of velvet ribbon to co-ordinate with your furnishings. Stitch the velvet ribbon around the edges of your front cushion piece over a plain-coloured fabric.

Children's ribbons can be stitched onto brightly-coloured cushions to brighten up a bedroom.

Ribbons tied in bows make an attractive finish for

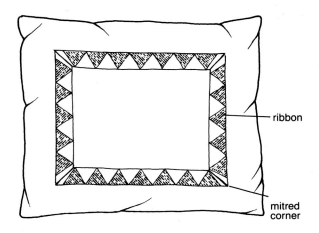

29 *Stitch ribbon to the front cushion pieces mitring the corners*

a cushion. Narrow satin ribbon can be cut into several small lengths, tied in short bows and stitched at random over the front of a cushion piece. Alternatively a wide floppy bow can be stitched to the centre or corner of a cushion and used for decorative purposes in a bedroom. Oddments of ribbon can also be used by stitching them in separate lengths to the front cushion piece covering the piece entirely. Machine stitch the lines of ribbon together overlapping them slightly (fig. 30).

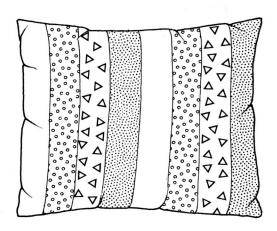

30 *Oddments of ribbon can be stitched together to cover the front cushion piece entirely*

BEADING

Beading is a very attactive way of making a cushion eye-catching. However, if your cushion is not purely for decoration then choose small beads and work them in the corners, or perhaps just one corner of your front piece so that it will not be uncomfortable to sit against. If your cushion is used solely for decoration then you can work a motif over the entire front area. Always design your motif on paper first. Alternatively you might like to use a rich dark-coloured velvet cloth and sew small glass beads at random onto the velvet background.

TASSELS AND FRINGING

Fringing can be sewn to the perimeter of the cushion to accentuate the shape of the cushion and to co-ordinate a room. The fringing is hand-sewn into position once the cover has been completed. Most types of fringing have a heading and it is this part which is sewn to the cushion.

Tassels can also be used to decorate cushions — they are most often used for trimming the ends of gathered bolsters. Tassels can also be stitched to the corners of a cushion, or stitched around the circular ends of a bolster.

BUTTONING

Buttoning is a traditional and popular way of finishing a cushion particularly in fabrics such as dralon and velvet. Make up your cushion and decide how many buttons you want to use for decoration. You may only require one in the centre or several positioned at random. Choose a button with a shank, you will need at least two, one either side of the cushion. Insert the needle through the cushion and through the shank of one button, then take the needle back through the cushion to secure the other shank in place. Use button thread for this type of work to prevent the thread snapping under stress.

If you prefer you can use a covered button to finish your cushion. To cover a button, first place it on your fabric, draw around the outside edge allowing an extra 1.5 cm (½ in). Cut the circle out and work a gathering stitch around the outside edge. Position the button on the wrong side of the cloth and draw up the thread so that the fabric over the button is quite tight. Keep the raw edges to the inside of the button and tie the ends securely to finish.

APPLIQUÉ

Appliquéd motifs can be used to echo the theme of a room. In a child's room, why not cut out motifs from curtain remnants, of their favourite television or cartoon characters for instance. When cutting out the motif allow a 1.5 cm (½ in) border around the edge. Press medium-weight iron-on Vilene to the

This bedroom throw is decorated with ribbon and a broderie anglaise frill. Pillow slips and quilted cushions match

wrong side of the motif to prevent it from fraying. When the Vilene is quite cold cut around the motif eliminating the 1.5 cm (½ in) border. Pin the motif to the right side of the cushion piece, using a plain-coloured fabric for the background, and then tack them in place. Either hand-sew or zig-zag the motifs in place.

Appliqué can also be used in other rooms. Cut out the central motif from curtain or loose cover remnants, using Vilene as a backing to prevent the edges fraying. Pin the motif to a corner or centre of your cushion, using a plain background to emphasize your motif and hand-sew or machine it in place. For very simple shapes add a hem allowance of 8 mm (³⁄₈ in) and, instead of using Vilene, baste all the raw edges into position on the wrong side of the cloth, before sewing them to the cushion cover. Appliqué can also be used for cutting out lace and stitching the motifs to a cushion cover for an effective trimming.

PATCHWORK

Small hand- or machine-sewn patchwork can be put to effective use on cushion covers. You can choose to make the entire cover in patchwork, just the front piece or use a central motif on a plain background. If your cushion is not purely for decoration machine-sewn patchwork is recommended. The simplest patchwork is different coloured squares sewn together. By incorporating scraps of curtain or loose cover fabrics into your patchwork the cover will co-ordinate with the room. If you want to create a less rigid effect cut out a number of paper shapes then re-arrange them until they fit the size of your cushion. This is known as a random patchwork design and should always be arranged on paper before cutting the different shapes out of fabric. One of the simplest types of patchwork is to use a central design on a plain background. Cut out seven hexagonal shapes and stitch them to the front cushion piece working on a plain-coloured background to emphasize the patchwork. This type of design could also be used for a set of squab cushions designed for dining-room chairs.

EMBROIDERY AND TAPESTRY

Small cushions make perfect samplers for embroidery. They can be used to decorate a baby's room, with the name and date of birth stitched onto the fabric. A small tapestry can be worked in the same way. Alternatively, a small tapestry can be set on a larger cushion by stitching it onto plain-coloured fabric and a narrow strip of ribbon hand-sewn around the edges of the tapestry to disguise the edges. Embroidery can be worked on pillow cases to identify his and her pillows. Or embroidered cushions can be arranged in a conservatory depicting flowers that can be found there. An attractive embroidered hanky could also be made up into a cushion cover provided it is stitched to a similar weight backing cloth. Old tablecloths that are no longer used but which have been worked with attractive designs can be cut up and used as cushion covers.

IRON-ON MOTIFS

For a very quick and simple method of decorating cushions, use a selection of iron-on motifs. There are soft furry animal shapes ideal for a nursery, or colourful cartoon characters and popular slogans for a teenager. For the bedroom use ready-made embroidered flowers that can be simply ironed into one corner of your cushion, then edged with co-ordinating ribbon to finish.

QUILTED CUSHIONS

Simple square cushions can be made more interesting if the surface has been quilted. If you haven't the time to quilt cloth but like the effect, then you can buy a small amount of ready-quilted fabric and perhaps use a piped border in bias binding of a contrasting colour.

To make quilted cushions you will need to make your paper pattern. Using the pattern cut out your main fabric twice, two pieces of wadding and two pieces of backing cloth. Using tailor's chalk and a rule draw out your pattern on the fabric pieces; lines running vertically and horizontally is the easiest type of quilting to begin with.

Take one fabric piece and, with the right side uppermost, place the wadding to the wrong side and the backing under the wadding. Pin all three layers of cloth together and tack the outer edges together to keep them in position. Machine along the chalk lines, using a quilting bar if you have one, then remove the tacking. Don't press quilting or it will loose its attractive plump appearance. Repeat this process with the remaining cushion pieces and then continue to make up the cushion using the method of your choice.

Once you have mastered the quilting technique you can then go on to stitch more elaborate patterns on your fabric. Alternatively, use patterned fabric and quilt around the motifs. Most types of fabric can be quilted but cottons are easier to handle; slippery cloths such as satins are more difficult and not to be recommended until you are proficient.

Cushions are such versatile furnishings that they can be used in virtually every room in the house.

IN THE BEDROOM

Cushions in a bedroom can range from under-pillow bolsters, pillow cases and window seats to decorative scatter cushions for the bed.

Pillow cases in plain-coloured cotton can be trimmed with lace that should be at least 5 cm (2 in) wide, and edged with narrow strips of satin ribbon. Strips of lace can either be incorporated into the side seams and applied in the same way as a frill, or they can be hand-sewn to the right side of the case once it has been completed. Lace and ribbon can also be worked in criss-cross or diagonal patterns over the front pillow piece. Select lace with a smooth surface or it will be too uncomfortable to sleep on. Take the right side of your front piece and pin strips of lace or ribbon in position, tack and then machine the strips in place working rows of stitching either side of the strips to ensure they lay flat.

Several different-sized cushions covered entirely with lace can be scattered around the head of the bed for decoration. Choose square, round or heart-shaped ones, make the inner cover in the usual way but use a backing fabric with lace or the inner cover will show through. If you want to emphasize the lace pattern choose a backing fabric in a contrasting colour. Cut out the backing fabric and your lace covering from your pattern, and then stitch the wrong side of the lace to the right side of the backing cloth before making up the cushion. To avoid the lace getting caught in a zip close the opening with a slip stitch. For a more co-ordinated look you may wish to use lace and backing cloth in the same colour.

A simple design worked in embroidery is another way to make an ordinary pillow case look special. Keep the design to the corners and edges of the pillow to avoid leaving an impression on your face while you sleep.

Pastel-coloured ribbons are a simple way of finishing the edges of a pillow or cushion. Once your cushion or pillow has been made up, measure enough ribbon to cover the perimeter. With wrong sides together press the ribbon in half lengthways. Slide the edges of the cushion or pillow into the ribbon so that it touches the crease line. Pin, tack and then machine the ribbon border in place.

For a more comfortable weekend lie-in, fix bedrest cushions above the bed. These are made from the box cushion pattern (see page 42) but two loops are stitched into the top welt seam. Cut two loops for each cushion 8×20 cm (3×8 in). With right sides together fold them in half lengthways and stitch along the length of the strip. Turn the

This bed has been transformed into a sofa with the addition of a two-tiered fitted cover and matching cushions in various shapes

loop to the right and press firmly. Pin the loops either side of the welt approximately 8 cm (3 in) in from the corner edge. Stitch the loops in place when you stitch the welt seams. The loops are then threaded onto a pole which is suspended above the bed.

Window seats are a good way of utilizing extra space. They are made from the box cushion pattern and filled with shallow pieces of foam between 4-6 cm (1½-2½ in) deep. Depending on the length of your sill it may be necessary to make more than one cushion. Window seats look particularly attractive when designed to co-ordinate with curtains and bedcovers.

Sweet-smelling herb cushions are a delightful way of making drawers fragrant. Small cushions can be made from cotton, lace or voile cut into hearts, circles or rectangles, edged with narrow strips of lace and filled with dried flowers or herbs. You might also like to slip a small bag of pot-pourri into a large cushion with the filling but remember to remove it before washing.

IN THE NURSERY

A child's room is definitely one area of the house where you can experiment with colour. The addition of one or two brightly-coloured floor cushions can be a focal point of the room and ideal for relaxing on or for props in imaginative play. These cushions should measure 90 cm (36 in) square and filled with foam chips. A tough washable cotton is most serviceable and all seams should be stitched twice for added strength. You could also make a sofa on the floor using square-shaped cushions to sit on and oblong shapes for the back part. Small children would also have plenty of fun with a long strip of foam covered using the box cushion method. This strip could be used for rolling around on, or, combined with a bolster, for a resting place for an afternoon nap.

Cushions in a child's room need to be fun. Furnishing fabrics depicting favourite cartoon or television characters will prove tremendously popular. Cushions for a playroom can also be made from fabric oddments, sewn together in blocks of different colours. Do remember that all fabrics for the nursery should be washable.

Cot bumpers

Cot bumpers are a practical way of protecting a baby from draughts. Bumpers are made in the same way as squab cushions and designed to a simple oblong shape. You can choose to line the entire cot or just the end where your baby sleeps. Bumpers are filled with wadding and held in place with ties fastened to the cot bars. To prevent toddlers undoing ties, replace them with shorter ones that are secured with poppers or Velcro.

Changing mat

An oblong of foam covered with PVC makes a handy changing mat for a baby. Make sure that it is wide and long enough for your baby to roll on and insert fabric ties at either end so that the mat can be rolled up and secured for travelling.

Pyjama cases

To entice young children to put their night clothes away a pyjama bag can be very useful. Make it from just a back and front piece with the opening in the back so that it is easier for the child to find. Decorate the case with an animal or doll's face using remnants of wool and cloth for trimmings. Do not use small buttons or beads.

IN THE BATHROOM

If you enjoy a long relaxing bath then a cushion for your head makes the experience more comfortable. Ready-made bath cushion pads are available from most department stores, or you can cut your own from foam. Cover the pad with a light quick-to-dry material such as polyester cotton and make it more attractive by adding a short frill to the outer edge.

A bath mat can be made from a cushion pattern. Draw it to an oblong or circle shape to the size you require, cover it with brightly-coloured towelling using a piece of foam for the filling. Appliqué a motif on the front section if desired.

IN THE DINING-ROOM

Make the seats of wooden chairs more comfortable by tying squab cushions to them. A washable fabric should be used so that the covers can be laundered frequently. If you want the ties on your dining chairs to be a focal point, use wide strips of ribbon and tie elaborate bows. Alternatively, add long narrow strips of ribbon and wind them in a criss-cross pattern three-quarters of the way down the chair leg tying them in a bow at the end.

Chests, workboxes and wooden stools can be used as impromptu seats by adding a box cushion. Choose a hard-wearing cloth that will withstand constant friction against a wooden surface. Instead of the box cushion design, make a cushion to fit without a welt and insert a frill into the seams, one long enough to reach the floor.

IN THE LIVING-ROOM

Unlike the dining-room where it is necessary to work with practical fabrics, the living-room can be the focus of more expensive materials that perhaps require the occasional dry-cleaning.

If you are furnishing on a budget you can make an inexpensive sofa by adding cushions to a simple wooden frame comprising slats of wood secured to a raised plinth.

Bolster cushions with tasselled trimmings, are an attractive way of making a large sofa more comfortable. They can also be used for dividing the sofa into separate seats. Make decorative cushions with large lengths of soft cotton or polyester crêpe de Chine material, tuck two sides in and then fold them onto the inner cushion. Take the remaining two ends and bring them to the centre and secure with a large bow or knot. Alternatively, cover a square cushion and tie lengths of ribbon around it to create a parcel effect securing the ribbon in the centre with a bow.

A rocking chair is more comfortable with squab cushions tied to the seat and back. If you wish you can make one long squab cushion but provide plenty of ties to prevent it from slipping.

IN THE GARDEN

You can make your own sun bed by simply covering a thick piece of foam using the box cushion method. Select a bright summery cotton cloth and one that will withstand plenty of hard wear. From a remnant of fabric you could also sew a simple square or round cushion to rest your head on.

A deck-chair with a cushioned lining looks more inviting than just canvas. Using the squab style of cushion, first measure the length of the canvas allowing for seams. Select a bright colourful cloth, perhaps a stripe or check pattern, and cut out a front and back piece. For decoration add a single or double frill, too. To keep the lining in place you might also like to add a flap for the top end of the chair, as for the pillow case.

Outdoor furniture tends to be rather basic and is made more comfortable by the addition of box cushions especially in bright primary colours. Squab cushions can be tied to cane furniture to make it more comfortable.

A HOME FOR ROVER

Dog and cat baskets can be expensive and your pet could be just as happy sleeping on a large sag bag floor cushion. This type of cushion moulds itself to the shape of the animal's body. Using the box cushion principle cut out your pattern to a round shape and the size you need. Then allow for a welt to a depth of at least 35 cm (14 in). Using a strong fabric, such as corduroy, denim or calico, sew the pieces together. Having made an inner cover fill it with polystyrene granules and slip stitch the opening to close it. It is advisable to make a second row of stitching around the inner cover to prevent the granules escaping. Fill the inner cover to three-quarters full to create a nice soft, squashy effect.

PART III

9 *LOOSE COVERS*

Loose covers are an inexpensive way of giving furniture a new lease of life, especially if you have acquired a second-hand bargain or a junk shop find. Although the prospect of making covers may seem quite daunting, the key to success lies in knowing how to measure-up for the pattern.

You can make loose covers for most styles of chair or sofa and, as their name implies, they have the advantage of being easy to remove for washing or dry cleaning.

Always work with furnishing and not dress fabrics which are not strong enough to withstand the constant wear-and-tear. Furnishing fabrics are also wider than dress fabrics and more economical. For your first project it is advisable to work with a plain fabric or one with an overall pattern. Fabrics with a large pattern have to be matched carefully and motifs need to be placed centrally on the furniture.

MEASURING UP

Taking the measurements for your loose cover pattern is the most crucial stage. You will need to be prepared to spend plenty of time ensuring that the measurements are exact – avoid working in a hurry. Loose covers require large quantities of fabric so always double check on the amount you need before you make a purchase.

Until you are experienced in making covers it is a wise precaution to make a calico pattern before you buy your fabric and certainly before you start cutting into it. If you make a calico pattern first, it gives you the opportunity to try it out on your seat and make any adjustments. Then you can lay the pattern out on an old sheet to the width of the fabric you intend to buy. Position the pattern pieces on the sheet, working with the grain line running in the same direction, so that you can calculate the amount of material you need. If you have a couple of discarded double sheets these can be used instead of calico. Any mistakes you make can then be rectified on the calico pattern instead of your fabric. When you take measurements do so from the widest point of each section. Make a brief sketch of your chair so that you can write in all the measurements as you take them. If your chair has a removable cushion seat take this out of position so that you can measure for the cover that sits underneath it, remembering to measure for the cushion, too.

If you are calculating the cost of covering a chair you can make a very rough total by estimating that you will need something in the region of five times the height of the back of the chair to the bottom edge.

At certain areas on your cover you will have to allow for a tuck-in. This is the extra piece of fabric, used at the back and sides of the chair, that helps to keep the cover in place. Also keep in mind that you will need extra cloth for covering the piping cord and perhaps an extra 50 cm (20 in) of cloth for any possible repairs later on. If you want matching cushions, arm caps and chair backs include them in your fabric measurements too. Arm caps and chair backs enable you to protect the areas of your cover that are likely to become heavily soiled and they can be washed and replaced without the entire cover having to be removed.

The seven main areas that you will need to measure are (fig. 31):

1 The outside back from the top of the chair to the bottom edge.

2 The inside back from the top of the chair to the base of the back piece, plus a 15 cm (6 in) tuck-in.

3 The seat area with a 15 cm (6 in) tuck-in either side and at the back edge.

4 The front of the seat.

5 The outside arm.*

6 The inside arm with a 15 cm (6 in) tuck-in.*

7 The front of the arm.*

*Double these measurements to allow for the two arms.

In addition to these measurements you should allow 2 cm (¾ in) for all the seams.

Finishing the bottom edge
You will also need to allow material for the type of finish you want on your chair. For a fitted look you can use a set of four flaps, one on each side of the chair, with ties attached that are tied in bows underneath the chair (fig. 32).

To measure for the flaps turn your chair upside down. Measure from the edge of the chair to 10 cm

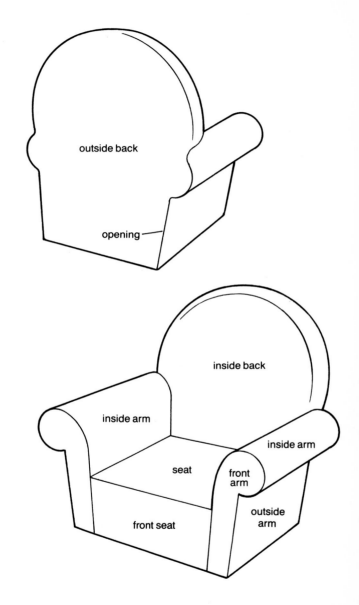

31 *Making the pattern for a loose cover of an armchair. The seven main areas to measure are shown below*

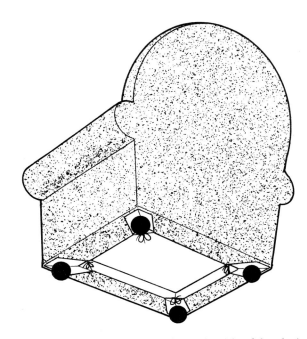

32 *Four flaps tied with bows on the underside of the chair provide a neat finish*

33 *A frill makes a decorative trimming on the loose cover for an armchair*

(4 in) beyond the leg, then measure the length of the side of the chair. Cut out the flaps, shaping them by tapering them slightly on each side. Make a double hem on each side edge and make a narrow 2 cm (¾ in) hem on the top edge incorporating the ties at either end. Flaps provide a simple uncluttered finish to the edge of a chair cover, but there are more decorative styles you can choose.

Provided you are working with a soft cloth then a frill makes a very decorative trimming (fig. 33). To determine the length of your frill take a piece of string and measure around the lower edge of the chair. For a soft fabric you will need twice this amount of fabric and for slightly firmer cloths use

one and a half times the amount. Measure the depth from the bottom edge of the front seat piece to the floor allowing for seams. Make up the frill and attach it to the cover using piping sandwiched between the frill and lower edges of the cover. For a contrasting effect you can encase the hem of the cover in binding or ribbon.

Box pleats are a popular way of trimming the lower edge of loose covers. Measure the bottom edge of the chair as described for a frill then multiply this amount by the size of pleat you intend to use. Pleats for chair covers tend to be about 12 cm (4¾ in) wide. To measure their height, measure from the bottom edge of the front seat piece to 5 mm (¼ in)

This sofa has a loose cover with a frilled edging and separately covered cushions. The cushion piping matches

from the floor (box pleats are usually made to sit slightly off the floor). You will need to see that the outside edge of the pleat sits neatly on the corner of the chair. You may have to juggle with the pleats in order to get them to sit in the right position, making the corner pleat slightly above or below 12 cm (4¾ in). By working on a strip of calico first you can avoid making your fabric grubby and simply transfer your markings when you have fitted the strip exactly in position.

Scallops make a very fancy trimming ideal for a bedroom chair. Measure the length of strip you need as described before, then measure the length of your scallop from bottom edge of the front seat piece to 5 mm (¼ in) from the floor. Again, you will need to juggle with scallops so that they sit neatly on the corner of the chair.

THE CALICO PATTERN

Always make a separate calico pattern for each item of furniture you cover. Store the calico so that you can use it for reference when your cover needs replacing. Don't unpick an old loose cover as it is likely to have shrunk in the wash. If you have bought a washable fabric it is worth taking the time to put it through your machine in case it shrinks. Having taken the measurements for the various sections of the chair, cut large rectangles of calico or sheeting that will encompass these measurements, remembering to allow for seams and tuck-ins.

Working on one area at a time place the pieces of calico over the chair securing them in place with upholstery pins or sticky tape. Carefully draw around the outline of the section you are working on, using a pencil. Remove the calico and cut around the pencilled outline, allowing 2 cm (¾ in) for seams. Place the calico pieces back on the chair to ensure that the pieces have been traced exactly. Continue making a calico pattern for each section of the chair including the type of finish you want along the bottom edge.

Assembling the pieces

Pin all the pieces together and then join them with tacking stitches, as the pins are liable to drop out when you fit the calico on the chair.

With so many pattern pieces to work with it is helpful to sew them together in a set order to ensure that each piece is stitched in the right place. Label each piece either by name or by number with french chalk to avoid confusion. Begin by stitching the back piece to the inside back, then the inside back to the seat area. Then stitch the seat to the panel at the front of the seat. Next, stitch the seat area to the arms along the inside edge, then the inside arm to the outside arm, then stitch the front of the arms in place. Stitch the end of the arm pieces to the back and inside back leaving an opening on one back seam of approximately 35 cm (13¾ in). Your opening should run from the bottom edge of the chair to the beginning of the scroll (curve) on the arm of the chair. Finish stitching by adding your trimming to the bottom edge, whether it is pleats, a frill or flaps.

Slip the calico onto the chair. On the curved areas, such as the front of the arms, it may be necessary to ease out a small amount of fullness. To do this unpick the tacking stitches and make tiny pleats or gathering stitches on the wrong side of the cloth. Once you have made your pleats or gathers tack the edges together again to ensure the pieces fit comfortably.

Once you are satisfied that your cover fits well take it off the chair and unpick all the tacking so that the calico is in pieces.

MAKING THE COVER

Having bought your fabric lay it out on the floor
with the right side facing you. Put the calico pieces
on it, checking that the grain is correct (fig. 34).
You may find it helpful to number all your pattern
pieces with chalk on the wrong side of the cloth to
ensure that you stitch them together in the correct
order. Also add a chalk arrow to indicate the top
and bottom edge of each piece. You could even write
the name of each section on the back. Sections that
need to be piped could be identified by a small cross
on the back. Once all the pattern pieces have been
marked cut them out.

Inserting piping

Areas of the loose cover that require piping are the
top edge of the front of the seat, the front arm
pieces, between the inside and outside arm pieces,
between the inside and outside back pieces along
the top edge and between the bottom edge of the
cover and the finishing trim. It isn't essential to use
piping, but it does strengthen the covers at the seam
areas and helps to exaggerate the outline of the
chair.

Attach the piping to the areas of the chair that
you have indicated, then stitch all the sections
together. Trim any bulky seams and clip around the
curved edges of the front arm pieces.

Fastenings for loose covers

The most durable type of fastening for covers are
hooks and eyes or Velcro. Although zips can provide
a neat inconspicuous finish they are not sufficiently
strong for loose covers, especially as the covers,
after they have been washed, need to be stretched
slightly to ease them back into place.

Neaten the chair opening with a double hem on

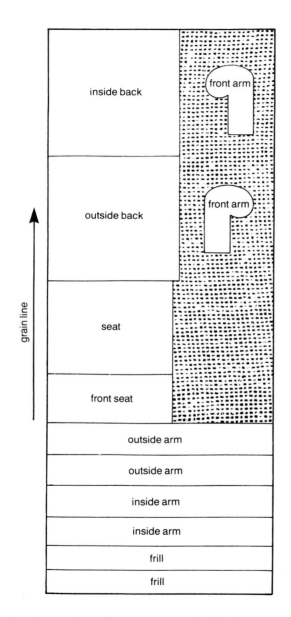

34 *Laying out the calico pieces onto the fabric*

the raw edges, sew hooks and eyes the length of the opening using a heavy duty cotton, sewing them approximately 12 cm (4¾ in) apart. Alternatively you can use strips of Velcro that should be machined rather than hand-sewn in place.

Finishing the flaps

If you have chosen to finish your chair with flaps you will need to neaten the remaining raw edges with a machined double hem. Incorporate ties made from strips of bias binding. You will need eight ties each 25 cm (10 in) long. The ties are secured in bows at each corner and should not be visible once the chair is in position.

Making arm caps and chair backs

If you have allowed sufficient material for arm caps they should be made for chairs and sofas. The pattern can be taken from the outline of the inside arm, outside arm and front arm pieces. The length of the cap should be two-thirds of the total length of the arm of the chair.

Using the calico pattern for the front arm piece cut off the head of the scroll allowing 1.5 cm (½ in) for a hem. Take the outside arm piece and measure down for 11 cm (4¼ in) plus seams and cut off at this point. With right sides together stitch the outside and inside arm pieces, using piping if you wish to, then add the front arm piece, again piping around the curved edge. Make a double hem on all the edges, and clip the curved area on the front arm piece (fig. 35).

To make a chair back cut a piece of fabric 30×38 cm (12×15 in). Hem all the raw edges mitring the corners. Lay the cloth on the chair with the extra 8 cm (3 in) on the longer edge taken over to the back of the chair to hold it in position.

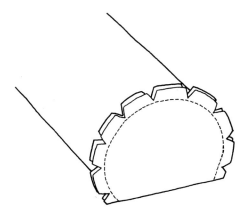

35 *Making an arm cap from the calico pieces, using the inside arm and the adapted front arm and outside arm pieces. The curved area on the front arm piece is clipped*

COVERING A SOFA

The same basic principles used when making a cover for a chair are used for a sofa. You will be working with twice as much fabric, so you need to allow plenty of room for cutting out and sewing the pieces together.

On a three-seater sofa it may be necessary to make seams in the back and seat pieces as these areas are very wide. If you have to allow for seams in the cover, position them so that the area is divided into thirds or perhaps a central seam. If your sofa has separate cushions you will need to ensure that the seams on the inside back sofa piece correspond with the seam edges on the cushions.

As longer flaps are required on the bottom of a sofa they can be neatly secured with one piece of cord rather than several ties. On the flap pieces make a narrow casing on the top edge about 2 cm (¾ in) deep. Take several metres of binding and attach a safety pin to one end, push the pin through

This living room is a blaze of matching blues. The cushions are highlighted with appliqué, frills, ribbon and single borders

the casing on all the flaps. Pull the cover over the sofa and turn the sofa upside down or on its side. Pull the bias binding until the flaps are neatly in place, then tie the two ends of the binding together.

Cushions for a sofa are made using the box cushion method and are fastened with a zip incorporated in the back welt piece.

COVERING A SUITE

If you are planning to cover a suite of furniture make a calico pattern for each piece first so that you can order sufficient fabric to cover them all. If you buy fabric for each item separately there is a chance that you will be buying from a different roll of fabric and the dye may be slightly different.

Even though two chairs may look identical it is worthwhile to make individual patterns for each one. Don't assume that one cover will fit the other, especially if you are covering old furniture. Always make your first project a chair rather than a sofa so that you can gain experience with a smaller area. If you have selected a patterned fabric with a central motif ensure that it sits in the same position on every piece of furniture.

Loose covers tend to be thought of in terms of a covering for a suite. However, there are a variety of other types of furniture that can be given a new image with a loose cover. Furniture not constantly in use can be covered with less practical dress fabrics and trimmed with elaborate bows, swags and ribbons.

A CHAIR WITHOUT ARMS

A smaller item of furniture such as a chair without arms is an ideal project for a beginner. It requires far less fabric than a sofa or armchair and fewer pattern pieces.

You will need to measure for a back, inside back, seat, front seat, side seat and any finishing trim you may want. If you want to disguise the legs you can use a frill or pleats (fig. 36). However, if the legs of the chair are to remain visible use flaps and tie them together underneath.

Although this type of cover is simpler than an armchair it is worthwhile making a calico pattern. Alternatively, you could use a paper pattern as the fitting stage is not so complicated. Allow for piping around the top and lower edge of the front seat and side pieces. You can also choose to pipe the back and inside back pieces along the side edges.

Begin by stitching the front seat part to the two sides. Stitch on the seat part incorporating the

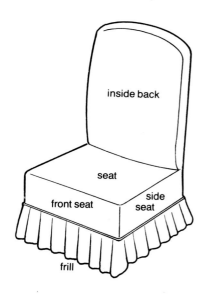

36   *Measuring for a chair without arms*

piping, stitch the inside back to the seat, then the back piece to the inside back and side ends. Take the cover and slip it on the chair and pin the finishing edge in place, marking the exact length you require. Make up the finishing edge and stitch it to the cover.

If your chair is rather worn then add a piece of foam cut to the exact size and shape of the chair. Simply place it on the chair and make up the cover.

Once the cover is in place it will keep the foam in position.

As a more decorative finish you can choose to neaten the side seams of the back and inside back pieces with a double hem. Then, stitch lengths of ribbon at intervals down the side of the chair tying them in bows once the cover is complete. This is suitable for bedroom furniture and the final touch is a deep frill round the lower edge. For a very stylish look, stitch one large bow to the back section of the chair, or tie one with wide strips of fabric stitched between the inside and outside back pieces.

A STOOL

Covering a stool whether it is for the bedroom or kitchen is a simple project to attempt. In the kitchen it may be advisable and more practical to add a round box cushion or a squab cushion with ties to the stool. However in the bedroom you can afford to be more impractical and use a long decorative frill.

To make a cover for a stool, first turn it upside down and trace around the top piece onto a sheet of paper. Cut around the shape allowing 1.5 cm (½ in) for seams. Cut a welt to the circumference of the top allowing for seams, then make up piping to twice the length of the welt. Stitch the welt to the circle of fabric inserting the piping. Place these pieces on the stool and measure for the length of the frill noting the exact length you require. Make up the finishing trim and stitch it to the lower edge of the welt piece incorporating the piping.

A DRESSING-TABLE

A prettily covered stool and dressing-table can be made the focal point in a bedroom. You could cover an old desk, small table or simply use a wooden shelf secured to the wall and adapt them as dressing-tables if you are working to a budget.

To get the exact dimensions of the top of your dressing-table a paper pattern is necessary, particularly for one that is kidney-shaped, in order to cut the curved shape correctly. Lightly tape the paper to your table and trace around the shape. If your dressing-table has a removable plate glass top then you can use this. Cut out your pattern, placing it on your fabric and allowing 1.5 cm (½ in) for seams. It is not necessary to think only in terms of furnishing fabrics for this type of cover as it will receive little wear and tear and lighter-weight dress fabrics are ideal.

Cut out the top cover for the table and line it with iron-on medium-weight Vilene for extra body. Alternatively, you could quilt this section of the cover. Neaten the back edge of the top cover piece with a double hem. Measure round the dressing-table for the frill omitting the back edge. Cut a strip of fabric to twice this measurement, noting the length you require. Neaten the side edges of the frill with a double hem and gather one longer edge. Pin the frill to the top easing out the gathers evenly and stitch in place. Fit the cover onto the table, check the length, then hem to the length you require.

If you have a dressing-table with a curtain track then you will need to attach a frill of just 15 cm (6 in) and make two separate curtains to hang onto the track.

Dressing-table covers can be decorated with bows stitched to the lower edge of the frill or the hem can be encased with ribbon binding and small bows stitched at random onto the frill. You might like to make the entire cover in lace or a soft satin fabric. The fabric you choose could also be used for making scatter cushions for the bed.

A BED

Although you are required to work with large pieces of fabric, making a cover for a bed or divan is very easy and is an ideal project for a beginner to learn the basic techniques of measuring and sewing covers. It is simply a rectangular piece of fabric edged with a frill or pleated trimming. You can choose to make your cover in a pretty fabric suitable for the bedroom or, if the bed doubles as a couch during the day, use a more practical cloth and decorate it with a variety of cushions.

Measure out the size of your bed and allow for seams. If your fabric is not wide enough to cover the width of your bed then choose either to have a centre seam or two seams with the area divided into thirds. Measure around the circumference of the top, but do not include the top edge of the bed. Make up a strip of fabric for the frill twice the circumference measurement and allowing for the depth which is measured from the top of the mattress to the floor. Make a double hem on the top edge of the cover piece to neaten. Then neaten the side and one longer edge of the frill piece with a double hem. Gather the remaining raw edge of the frill and pin it to the cover, allowing slightly more gathers at the corners. Stitch the frill to the cover. For a more fitted effect use ready-quilted fabric for the top cover piece, unquilted fabric for the frill, and contrasting piping sandwiched into the top edge of the frill.

Informal throwover covers are ideal and distinctive as bed covers. Experiment with favourite shades and designs which pick up decorative themes from the rest of the room, or select a colour which contrasts with its surrounds to dramatic effect. Scalloped, tassled or even pleated frills make ideal edgings for this type of bed covering.

A DIVAN

A divan is covered using the same principle as the box cushion, although there is no zip or fastening required. If you prefer the divan can be piped to emphasize the shape. This treatment, particularly

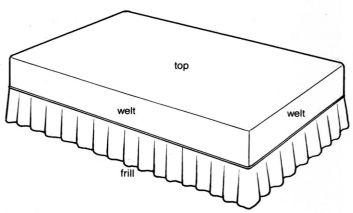

37 *Covering a divan*

with the addition of matching box cushions, will turn your divan into a comfortable day time sofa.

Begin by taking the measurements for the top of the divan allowing for seams on each side. Then measure the depth of the mattress allowing for two seams, then measure the length of the mattress plus a seam allowance. Measure for the frill from the lower edge of the mattress to the floor allowing for seams (fig. 37).

Join the edges of the welt together and press the seam open. Then stitch one edge of the welt to the top of the divan inserting piping if you wish. Stitch the ends of the frill together and neaten one longer edge with a double hem. Work a row of gathering stitches inside the seam allowance on the remaining raw edge of the frill. Pin the frill to the remaining

A simple, lightly pleated valance sets off the more elaborate but similarly coloured duvet cover

raw edge of the welt, easing gathers around evenly and inserting piping.

For a more formal room the lower edge of the cover, known as the valance, can be made from strips of fabric with a pleat at each corner. To calculate the amount of fabric you will need use the length measurement taken for the welt plus four times the depth of each pleat.

As a divan cover requires a considerable amount of fabric either design your cover so that seams are made at each corner, or so that they are concealed in the side edges.

11 THROWOVER COVERS

If you want to transform the appearance of your furniture instantly and you are short of time, then a throwover cover is the answer. Throwover covers, often referred to as throws, are also an attractive alternative to loose covers if your sewing skills are rather limited.

Throws can be used to cover beds, tables, chairs and sofas. Because we have been conditioned to accept that covers on chairs should be fitted it may take a little while to get used to this type of covering. You need to be bold about using fabric, arranging the cloth and then leaving it alone, resisting the temptation to constantly pull it about!

FABRICS

If your throw is for purely decorative purposes, such as a covering for a table or bed, then you can select a lightweight cloth. Bulky fabrics would be too difficult to arrange neatly over a table or dressing-table surface. Furnishing fabrics are a good choice because they are wide and they avoid the need for too many seams, but dress fabrics will provide you with a much greater variety of patterns and textures.

Lightweight fabrics are suitable for chairs and sofas provided they are not going to receive too much wear. A suite used for every-day purposes should be draped with a firmer linen or cotton. Cane and wood furniture needs to have some sort of padded covering or it will be too uncomfortable.

Soft woollen blankets can also be used as throws. You could stitch contrasting braiding to the outside edge for an attractive finish. Shawls with heavily fringed edges can also look very attractive casually draped, or perhaps partially covering a chair or sofa. A brightly-coloured sleeping bag, unzipped and placed over a chair or sofa, could also make a versatile covering. Appliquéd cot quilts are ideal for children's rooms draped over chairs or the centre of the bed. Old tablecloths with embroidery would make a lovely throw for a small chair or stool, and an antique bedcover with lace edging could be used on a sofa. If you want to create a nostalgic look by using antique or old-fashioned materials do have them cleaned first, repair any small tears and deal with any obvious stains or they will detract from the appeal of this type of cover. A quilt would make a lovely squashy cover for a dilapidated sofa and you could decorate it with an assortment of scatter cushions.

You need not only think in terms of using just one fabric, for example two or three shawls thrown together over a sofa could create a very dramatic effect. Or several floral prints draped together might be far more interesting than just one. The main point to remember when you are using more than one cloth is that they blend together. Fabrics should not fight with each other, rather they should blend together giving a casual but deliberately co-ordinated effect. It is not necessary to stitch lengths of fabric together – they can be draped on top of each other.

MAKING THE THROW

To cover your furniture with a throw you will need to decide whether you want to partially or entirely cover it. If you choose to cover the furniture entirely then you will need to use several metres of fabric. Partially covering a chair is fine provided the chair itself is still in a reasonable condition. A thread-bare cover, with stuffing showing through, and left showing when the chair is only half covered, will look most unattractive. If only one area of your chair is worn then you can use your throw to conceal it. If the chair is worn all over then you will need to use a sufficiently large throw to cover it completely.

With a young active family it might be more practical to use a throw to cover your furniture completely. You might otherwise find yourself constantly re-arranging your throw while young ones wriggle and put it out of position.

To decide just how much cloth you will need take an old sheet and drape it over your chair or sofa. Allow for enough material so that it can be tucked in at the back of the seat and the inside arm areas. This will help to keep the throw in place. You will then need to have enough cloth to take over the back of the chair and touch the ground and enough to drape over the arms and onto the floor if you wish. Use another sheet if you are running out of cloth pinning them together before laying them over the chair again. With young children about it might be advisable to seam separate lengths of cloth together. Once you have covered your chair or sofa remove the sheet and measure out the amount of fabric you will need.

Before placing your cover in position you may like to neaten the edges. You can simply pink the edges of the fabric if you wish. This type of finish is suitable for thick wool fabrics that are unlikely to fray or for felt. However, most household materials are liable to fray especially during washing so it is advisable to neaten the edges of the cloth. If you really are short on time then you can stick the hems of the throw in place with an adhesive hemming tape from Vilene. A stitched hem is stronger than a glued one and you simply need to make a double hem on each edge mitring the corners for a neat finish.

Ties and fastenings

If you want to emphasize the design of an attractively curved chair or one with scroll arms then the addition of a few ties and careful draping of the fabric will make this possible even on a throw. You can reveal the shape of the arms by pleating layers of fabric around it and making a few running stitches to hold those pleats in position. Pleating can also be used along the back area of the chair at either side. Take a small quantity of fabric in each hand, make a pleat by folding the cloth in your hand then pinning it. Attach ties made from strips of bias binding or narrow satin ribbon at intervals down the side of the chair to hold the pleats together. On geometric or broad striped patterns you might like to use press-on fasteners for a more modern finish.

COVERING A BED

Because a fitted bedcover involves using large quantities of fabric and attaching a frill or pleated edging, using a throw on a bed can minimize that

This table is disguised with two throws in contrasting colours. The theme is emphasized by matching blue and cream chair cushions

amount of work. If the frame of your bed is in good condition you may simply like to use a pretty piece of fabric and lay it diagonally over and not worry whether it touches the floor. This type of throw is suitable for a low bed. Ready-quilted fabric is ideal for bedding as it provides an attractive and warm cover and the edges of the quilting can be finished with strips of wide bias binding or ribbon to prevent them fraying.

If your room is decorated with several items of wooden furniture then a tartan rug with a fringed edging would help to convey a rustic look. Samples of patchwork also make suitable throws for a bed, while smaller samples can be used as cot throws in a child's room. An old fur coat or piece of fake fur fabric could also be used for throwing over a bed to create a cosy atmosphere.

Before measuring for the amount of fabric you will need for your throw, you will have to decide whether you want the cover to touch the floor or end just below the mattress. Although a throw designed to touch the ground looks very neat you may want to make a feature of some attractively carved legs on your bed.

Take your tape and measure from the centre of the bed to the floor or end of the mattress, then double this amount to give you the width of the throw. Then, measure from the floor at the end of the bed to the head of the bed for the length, allowing for hems on all the edges. If you want to be able to secure the throw in place by tucking it under the top edge of the pillow add an extra 20 cm (8 in) to the length measurement. If your fabric is not sufficiently wide to cover your bed then you can choose to make a centre seam or divide the area into thirds making two seams. Neaten the edges of the throw with a double hem and place it in position.

VERSATILE THROWS

Throws can be used throughout the house. Small circles or rectangles of fabric can be used to cover fancy tables, pianos, stools, in fact most items of furniture that have seen better days. Quilted throws once discarded from the bedroom or sofa can be folded into a square and used as an extra cushion, quilted fabric can also be used as an impromptu playmat for a young child on a vinyl or wooden floor.

If you order twice the amount of fabric you need for your throw you can use the second length for decorating walls. Use cloth with an interesting texture or intricate pattern. Secure the cloth to the wall by stapling it to wooden battens which are then screwed to the wall. This type of furnishing is suitable for a lounge or bedroom. In a child's bedroom a bright jazzy print could be used over the bed and repeated with the separate throw secured above the head of the bed.

By taking a couple of lengths of cloth and walking around the house you can begin to discover areas that can be covered. Try the fabric in all sorts of places, making a few pleats or folds where necessary, and you will begin to realize that the possibilities for using this type of cover are endless. Surfaces in a child's room or kitchen could be draped with PVC that requires no hemming. An over-stuffed chair can look quite luxurious draped with a velvet curtain or a shawl with a Paisley pattern.

Using throws means looking at your furniture in a new light and accepting that covers do not have to be formal and very fitted. It means you can act on impulse if you fall in love with a remnant — it is easy enough to find something to cover in the house!

ACKNOWLEDGEMENTS

The author and publishers would like to thank the
following for supplying photographs:
Bill Batten, page 71; Colefax and Fowler, page 10;
Crown Paints, page 47; Deschamps, from a
selection of fabrics and bed linen designed by
Primrose Bordier, back jacket; Harrison Drape,
page 67; ICI Fabrics, pages 27 and 34; Interior
Selection, front jacket, and pages 51 and 62;
London Interior Design Centre, page 71; Poppy
Ltd, Yarm, Cleveland, page 23; Syndication
International/Homes & Gardens, page 14; Warner
Fabrics, from their Claremont Collection, page 58;
World of Interiors, page 71; Brian Yates Interiors,
from the Silverdale Collection, page 39.

INDEX

Page numbers in *italics* refer to diagrams and illustrations